Bedrooms

Chris Casson Madden

Bedrooms

Creating the Stylish, Comfortable
Room of Your Dreams

PHOTOGRAPHS BY
Nancy E. Hill

EDITORIAL/STYLING ASSISTANCE BY
Carolyn Schultz AND Leslie Tucker

CLARKSON POTTER/PUBLISHERS · NEW YORK

Published by Clarkson Potter/Publishers, New York,
New York. Member of the Crown Publishing Group.

Random House, Inc. New York, Toronto, London,
Sydney, Auckland
www.randomhouse.com

CLARKSON N. POTTER is a trademark and POTTER and
colophon are registered trademarks of Random House, Inc.

Printed in the USA

Design by Douglas Turshen

All of the photographs in this book are by
Nancy Elizabeth Hill except for those on pages 44–45 and
56–61, which are by Peter Margonelli.

Library of Congress Cataloging-in-Publication Data
Madden, Chris Casson.
    Bedrooms / by Chris Casson Madden.—1st ed.
    Includes index.
    1. Bedrooms.   2. Interior decoration.
NK2117.B4 M33   2001
747.7'7—dc21   00-068809

ISBN 0-609-60749-9

10 9 8 7 6 5 4 3 2 1

First Edition

acknowledgments

THIS BOOK IS DEDICATED TO my parents, Ed and Ann; my brothers and sisters, especially my sister Mary, who shared my earliest bedroom and its memories with me. And special thanks to the guys in my life: Nick, Patrick, and of course Kevin, who assisted in every step of this book.

A big hug of gratitude for my incredible team who helped pull this book together for me, and never lost sight of my vision: Nancy Hill, a gentle and visionary photographer with a flawless eye; Carolyn Schultz, a stylist and writer of incomparable talent; and of course Leslie Tucker, who jumped in feet first and not only wrote and styled but kept us going forward on the road. Kudos also to my office manager, Agnes Rethy, and our intern, Jennifer Distasio, whose administrative help in the office was greatly appreciated.

A huge thank-you to the creative team at Clarkson Potter. Without their guidance, direction, and encouragement, *Bedrooms* would have been just an idea. To Annetta Hanna, my extraordinary editor, for once again giving me the freedom to pursue my dreams. To editorial director Lauren Shakely and publisher Chip Gibson, both of whom continue to believe in my vision and give me free rein to bring it to the printed page. Vanessa Hughes, Liz Royles, and Jaime Gass always returned and fielded the numerous phone calls, requests, and questions that emanate from my office. To Doug Turshen, Nora Negron, and MarySarah Quinn, whose artistic talent and energy are displayed on each and every page. To Barbara Marks, whose influence goes far beyond marketing and publicity and who takes such super care of me on my whirlwind book tours. And to the other members of a strong team who add their support before and long after publication: Andy Martin, June Zimmerman, Maha Khalil, Camille Smith, Joan Denman, and Maggie Hinders.

To all the designers who went beyond the call of duty to take care of my crew, especially Sarah Smith; Ellie Cullman and her assistant, Amanda; Cindy Rinfret; Helene Verin; Jamie Drake; Penny Drue Baird. And to Karen Houghton, Barrie Vanderpoel, Stephanie Stokes, Mark Finlay, Toni Gallagher, Arlene Pilson, Chris Coleman, Matthew Smyth, Glenn Gissler, Sandy Morgan, and James and Jennifer D'Auria. And to the more than gracious homeowners we encountered along the way, who shared their most personal space: Bob Sweet, Debbie and Phil Palazzo, Joanne Furey, and Karen and Bill Tell. To Jean Best for cooking soul food for us after many long shoot days and to Ric "the weather guru" for being our unofficial weatherman so we didn't photograph without the sun shining.

To the helpful staff at Twin Farms Inn: Beverley, Kelly, and Anne, who helped us photograph four of the beautiful bedrooms on the following pages. And to Mac Hoak for his understanding when we took over the grounds of his wonderful shop, Mecox Gardens, one hot, sunny afternoon.

To Danielle, Mia, Spencer, Taylor, Philip, Benjamin, and Nick for letting a bunch of adults take over their bedrooms for a day.

To the generosity of Joe Dance (Crate & Barrel), Connie Dankmyer (Nellie's of Amagansett), Kathy Yarbrough (Crown Craft), and Porthault for the use of props and for coming through at the last minute.

To Kim Kimball of Manchester, Vermont, and Rob and Robin Fariel at the Seabreeze Inn in Amagansett, Long Island, for providing wonderful accommodations for a tired and hardworking crew.

To Florence Hill, Venetta Williams, and Charles for providing child care while our dedicated photographer spent many a night away from home and, of course, William and Montgomery. To Andy, Mia, Claire, and Brandon Schultz for taking care of one another and for understanding when their mom had to be away.

To Rob Spilman and Matt Johnson for allowing me to design my dream bed and for marketing it throughout America.

To Tom Molloy, Judy Huebener, Abby Secoy, Mary Farrell, and Karen Peterson for their hard work in preparing my home in Vermont for photography and comfortable living.

To the librarians at the Cooper-Hewitt Museum who are always there to answer questions about the most abstruse points in design.

And to Winnie, Lily aka Lola, Charlie, Emma, Wallis, and Winston for providing a smile.

contents

introduction

I FONDLY REMEMBER MY FIRST BEDROOM, and I imagine most of you recall yours that way too. Mine was done in turquoise and lavender, and my prized accessory was a turquoise princess phone—nonworking model, of course. When my younger sister, Mary, became my roommate when I was eight, I negotiated a black-and-white oversize-tile floor from my parents and added touches of red to give the room a bit of texture. I wouldn't go with that decorating scheme again, but at the time, that bedroom was my pride and joy.

The bedroom probably reflects our deepest passions and our abiding interests more than any other room. Not that we don't create stylish and inspiring kitchens, bathrooms, living rooms, dining rooms, and libraries in our homes—we do, and we do so with great dedication, vision, and panache.

But the bedrooms that we craft for ourselves, our children, and our guests resonate deep within us. These spaces are special; uniquely ours.

As I traveled around the country scouting potential sites for *Bedrooms*, I marveled at the seemingly endless range of bedroom styles—from modern to country, from over-the-top to sweet and simple. I was struck by the multitude of dual uses that we find for bedrooms today—as media rooms, exercise rooms, home offices, and so on.

I discovered a fresh approach to children's rooms, from toddler to teenager. A new breed of designer—like Cindy Rinfret in Greenwich, Connecticut, and Penny Drue Baird in New York City; lots of names come to mind—devote a substantial portion of their practice to kids' rooms. The results are exciting and inspiring.

Talented architects like James D'Auria in New York have turned their considerable skills to designing memorable bedrooms, like the Tuscan-influenced one D'Auria shares with his wife, Jennifer, in Amagansett. My good friend Sarah

Smith, a top designer in New York, has completed a number of exciting projects on a small island off the Connecticut coast where she has summered for years. Sarah's skilled and sensitive touch has produced wonderful and varied bedrooms, which I was privileged to photograph with my team.

Sometimes a great hotel or inn can supply us with the inspiration to redecorate or restyle a room. The Mayflower Inn in Washington, Connecticut, for instance, inspired me to redo our guest room at home in the style of our room at that memorable inn. For *Bedrooms,* I was able to photograph four special bedrooms at Twin Farms, a top-rated inn in Barnard, Vermont. These rooms, in addition to being wonderful to look at, might very well give you the spark of an idea to begin your bedroom renovation.

I find design inspiration everywhere—in books, magazines, designer showcase houses, antique and decorative shops, and museums, at tag sales, on beach walks, and in a host of other places. A visit to Mecox Gardens in Southampton, New York, prompted me to ask owner Mac Hoak if I could photograph a charming shed that he had decorated with furniture and objects. I found it gave me some inspiring design ideas and strategies. I hope you'll have a similar experience.

This book covers a wide spectrum of decorating approaches for your bedroom. I hope it will be a source of inspiration for you, your family, your friends, and your guests.

Romantic Elegance

REFLECTIVE TRAVELS

Interior designer Karen Houghton and her husband, Michael, who is a dealer in rare and out-of-print books, are very much a part of the fabric of Nyack, New York. This small town on the Hudson River, an hour outside of New York City, is home to many well-known members of the art and theater worlds. The Houghtons' Second Empire Victorian house, built around 1850, is located in downtown Nyack, a favorite weekend haunt for antique and collectibles aficionados.

Houghton's passion for antiques began when, as a child, she would tag along on treasure hunts with her parents, who were antique dealers in Nyack in the 1960s. As she explains, "Finding an object that spoke to me, striking the deal, cleaning and mending it, looking it up in my reference books, and trying to evaluate its market value—this is the process I learned from my parents and still follow today. I love to collect, but now I spend more time helping my clients develop their own collecting passions. At

ABOVE A typical Houghton tablescape includes myriad textures and elements. Here, an antique milk glass with a heron motif is combined with a brass lamp, a silk tassel, and a green ironstone vase that holds roses from the garden. OPPOSITE Botanical specimens from a Smith College botany notebook, circa 1900, are framed and hung around an antique gilded mirror.

LEFT A twentieth-century Swedish country
bed is tucked into the sleeping niche
and is dressed with an array of textiles,
including an antique French Boutis quilt
of gold-colored silk, Cowtan & Tout fabric
pillows, and a white matelassé coverlet.
An antique opaline lamp provides reading
light beside the bed.

this point, my house is nearly full; it cannot accommodate more."

Houghton finds many pieces on the shopping trips she
takes to Europe at least twice a year. "I have my lucky haunts
in London and in the States that I return to regularly, but it
is such fun to venture down some unknown road and dis-
cover something delightful!" Her own master bedroom is the
perfect home for some of her many unique finds.

The couple's timelessly serene bedroom is filled with a
mixture of these pieces along with those she inherited from
her parents. She notes, "Since our bedroom is an odd shape,
I placed the sofa on an angle. This rounds out the corner and
allows the eye to travel across the room."

The alcove, original to the room, is the ideal spot for the
bed. Karen has deliberately kept to a warm, earthy palette
with touches of gilt throughout the space. The bed itself is
crowned with a gilt *ciel de lit*. And at the foot of the bed,
stacked atop one another, are a papered box, a gout stool, an
antique tooled metal-and-wood document box, and a
nineteenth-century Anglo-Indian camphor-wood box.

Says Houghton, "My boxes and baskets offer perfect
storage for many of my collections. They are wonderful in
themselves, and they can often be found for reasonable prices
at flea markets and antique stores."

Opposite the bed alcove is a niche that holds more baskets and boxes. These are filled with antique French and
American quilts. A nineteenth-century dressing table with
crystal knobs and its original Carrara marble top is the perfect setting for another collection—Karen's vintage perfume

RIGHT A 1930s lingerie "doll" hangs on the closet door, stuffed with a silk nightie. The framed antique prints above the vanity were found in eighteenth-century catalogs and books. BELOW Family pictures in ornate frames add a personal touch in the seating area. OPPOSITE A rich floral fabric on the upholstered chair is juxtaposed with a soft needlepoint carpet underneath.

bottles. The vanity is a rarity, she says, because she found it in its original condition without pieces missing. A strictly feminine touch is added by the prints above the vanity. The prints are from an eighteenth-century Parisian cosmetics catalog, and three more reflect one of her most recent passions —portraits of nineteenth-century women.

The enthusiasms of Houghton's husband are also reflected in this room. "Being the wife of a bookseller has its consequences," she says. "Almost all of the rooms and even our hallways contain books and bookshelves, so naturally we added a niche beside the bed to hold books as well."

Besides being the perfect place to settle in with a good read, this bedroom is a stylish nod to both of its occupants. "I can walk into this room again and again and not get tired of it," Houghton muses. "It feels good to wake up here."

MANHATTAN ROMANCE

Barrie Vanderpoel is a principal at Vanderpoel Schneider Group, an interior design firm. Vanderpoel, who lives in Manhattan with her husband, Wynant, has completed numerous bedroom projects for her clients, but her bedroom is very much her own, reflecting her love of beautiful textiles, antiques, and those objects that personalize a room, like good books, photographs of friends and family, heirlooms, and travel mementos.

A canopied bed, circa 1785, draped in a white fabric by Lee Jofa, is the focal point of the room. "I really love eighteenth-century furniture," she says. "Things that have been considered beautiful for three hundred years usually turn out to be pretty good choices."

Vanderpoel has chosen pristine white sheets from Monica Noel that have a tailored trim of green. At the foot of the bed, an upholstered custom-made bench by Lewis Mittman is covered in the Old World Weavers fabric "Piona," which is also used to upholster the walls and drape the windows. She has given definition to the room by outlining the arches, doors, and some of the furniture

OPPOSITE The skirted table conceals drawers for extra storage in this vanity designed by Vanderpoel. Electrified candlestick lamps flank a nineteenth-century mirror. ABOVE A Victorian tortoiseshell, crystal, and silver dressing set adds glamour and romance to the vanity. A silver mint julep cup holds a fresh bouquet.

with deep green grosgrain ribbon, which she simply glued on.

On her husband's side of the bed, on a small eighteenth-century wooden table, Vanderpoel has amassed a still life of necessities: a telephone, an orchid, and some framed photographs. She stores her magazines and newspapers underneath the table in two baskets. Vanderpoel notes, "I keep using these baskets because the proportions are so good."

At her bedside is a skirted glass-top circular table topped with a Steuben bird the Vanderpoels received as a wedding gift, along with two favorite family photographs and, always, a vase of fresh white roses.

At the top of Wynant's wish list for the bedroom was a large-screen television set easily visible from the bed. Barrie chose an armoire that she says, is "like great classic architecture."

Vanderpoel also added a piece that she feels, "adds a softness, a femininity, to the room." This is a dressing table that she designed and skirted. The lamps atop the dressing table are nineteenth-century English porcelain candlesticks she had wired, and the mirror is a reproduction Chippendale that Barrie found and whose frame she painted white. "I like elaborate pieces painted white to be more informal," she explains.

One piece that the designer created for herself over a decade ago and that she keeps re-creating for her clients is her floral-painted screen. "It's good for concealing things," she says. She puts hers to good use in front of a file cabinet full of materials for "late-night inspiration."

Throughout the room are carefully placed personal objects that are important to the Vanderpoels. Observes Vanderpoel, "I love anything that makes a room more personal. A room is a living thing. If you can't put your feet up on a table and display your favorite photos and prints and books, it has no life."

OPPOSITE An antique four-poster canopy bed is draped in a sheer cotton batiste. A white cashmere throw offers additional luxury to the upholstered bench. TOP A rare botanical print occupies the fabric-lined niche above the built-in cupboard. Grosgrain ribbon outlines the area for added architectural punch. ABOVE The signature Vanderpoel floral-painted screen conceals a file cabinet. The cupboard contains a collection of CDs and family photographs.

GREEN MOUNTAIN ELEGANCE

Once you've slept in a king-size bed, I was told, you may find it difficult—some say even traumatic—to return to a queen-size or a double bed. I have to say I wholeheartedly agree after spending the last year in our Vermont house in the king-size canopy bed that I designed for my furniture collection. It's a luxury for my husband and me to have that extra room for spreading out books and newspapers and my Saturday-morning breakfast tray, and it certainly makes it easier to accommodate our two dogs, Lola and Winnie, when they are allowed up on the bed.

Our home in Vermont is a casual place, a place meant to be lived in and comfortable. In dramatic contrast to the rugged greenery and hills outside our windows, the walls in our bedroom are painted a soft whipped cream, since serenity was paramount for me here. The four-poster bed, with its peach-patterned sheets from Palais Royal, is finished in a rich distressed cherry and topped with acorn finials. I have dressed the bed with layer upon layer of pillows, including standard, king-size, and small

ABOVE It is difficult to linger in bed on a beautiful day when breakfast is set up on the terrace and the sunshine is tempered by a lovely breeze. OPPOSITE The dark, oversize bed and large, round mirror make a strong architectural statement against the creams and whites of the room.

TOP Objects from my
travels, postcards,
and family pictures fill
the nooks and spaces
in my Cathay secretary.
ABOVE A fruitwood
dresser doubles as a
bedside table. It is
topped with a practical
slab of tierra marble.
RIGHT Perfect for quilts,
extra pillows, and
dogs, the bench at the
end of the bed is both
beautiful and useful.

The light in this room reminds

decorative boudoir pillows that I have collected over the years. I've also added some nineteenth-century faded floral cushions from France, a present from my dear friend, design maven Lynn von Kersting. At the foot of our bed is an upholstered bench—the original of which I discovered in a château in France; just like my four-poster bed, the bench has become part of my furniture collection.

Early morning sunlight streams in through our wrap-around deck, which is adjacent to the bedroom. In warm weather, this is the perfect spot for an intimate breakfast or, with its 360-degree mountain views, it can become a transcendental yoga platform.

Our spacious bedroom could have accommodated several "activity zones." But in keeping with my need for a calming Zen-like space, I have tried to furnish it with only a few select pieces. I have to confess, however, that my chinoiserie Cathay secretary is overflowing with small treasures and family photos.

Of course, the cozy, relaxing chaise longue that is placed next to our marble

fireplace is one of my special pieces; it's perfect for afternoon reading and relaxing during winter weekends in Vermont. Because the light in this room reminds me of my favorite city in the world, Venice, I surround the Cathay secretary with my dramatic collection of black-and-white photographs of early dawn in that great city, taken by the late renowned art director Alex Gotfryd. Unifying the room throughout is a taupe wall-to-wall carpet, warm in the winter and cooling in the summer.

Whenever we escape to Vermont for a weekend, I'm re-invigorated when I enter this room. It reflects in a very tangible way my passions—family, travel, and great design.

OPPOSITE An antique writing table fills a sunny spot in front of a narrow window in my dressing room. It is a lovely, private place to read the morning mail with my second cup of coffee. ABOVE Part of my collection of pillows, a mix of antique and handworked, finds a home on the cozy chaise longue.

REFINED COUNTRY

For this large master suite in the country, designer Stephanie Stokes recalls finding her inspiration in "the space itself—its generous size and high ceilings." Her clients—he is a busy executive who commutes daily to New York City, and she is an active member of the community and the mother of two children—had a wish list for their master bedroom: they wanted serious exercise equipment, a large-screen television, and an attached bath, all properly utilizing the generous space of the bedroom. And said the wife, "I wanted a romantic, feminine feel."

Stokes always listens very carefully to her clients' desires for their bedrooms. "People today spend the most time at home in their master bedrooms, so it is a critical room. It must be extremely beautiful and at the same time functional." She has a checklist of design requirements for all of her bedroom projects: good light for reading, great sheets ("I always look forward to coming home to my sheets," she says), a romantic bed, and a classic dressing table. Of paramount importance to all the spaces

ABOVE A simple still life offers elegant balance and proportion on the Colonial-style mantelpiece. OPPOSITE A bouquet of blue hydrangeas on the bedside table mirrors the chintz by Cowtan & Tout. The corona canopy fits the scale of the high, slanted ceiling while breaking dramatically into the large white space.

Stokes creates is a special sense of intimacy and privacy.

For this master bedroom, Stokes selected a vibrant yellow as the primary color. It is a color that had not been used in other rooms in the house and, as she notes, "the room gets lots of sun, and yellow is such a happy, sunny color."

Because the ceiling above the head of the bed is slanted, the use of a canopy presented a structural problem, but Stokes cleverly solved it by mounting a corona-shaped frame on the wall and draping it in an elegant beige fabric from Cowtan & Tout.

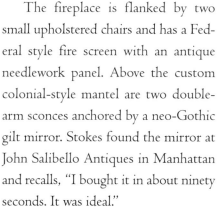

The fireplace is flanked by two small upholstered chairs and has a Federal style fire screen with an antique needlework panel. Above the custom colonial-style mantel are two double-arm sconces anchored by a neo-Gothic gilt mirror. Stokes found the mirror at John Salibello Antiques in Manhattan and recalls, "I bought it in about ninety seconds. It was ideal."

The exercise studio, which is just off the master bedroom, is furnished with state-of-the-art equipment, including a punching bag, a weight bench, a treadmill, and an exercise bike. "We treated each room separately, as there was a doorway between them, and chose the colors based on the master bedroom's chintz, but we deliberately kept this room quiet and subdued." Stokes painted the walls in the studio the same yellow as the master bedroom and added a coordinating hunter-green-and-yellow carpet. For the windows, she selected shades to cut the glare, and over them added a tailored Roman window treatment in a hunter-green-and-yellow plaid. About their exercise room, the wife said, "We wanted the gym to be close to our bedroom so we could work out anytime."

TOP The scale of the room allowed for many diverse pieces of furniture and generous use of the chintz fabric. ABOVE Egyptian cotton sheets, smooth chintz, and rich silk tassels on the canopy border incorporate luxury. OPPOSITE Sconces offer a soft ambient glow on the glazed yellow walls. The exercise room is part of the suite.

HARBOR VIEWS

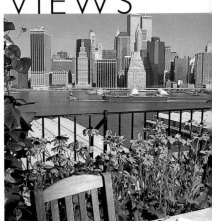

Across New York's Brooklyn Bridge lies the storied neighborhood of Brooklyn Heights. Home to artists, writers, and professionals who work in Manhattan, Brooklyn Heights is known for its distinctive architecture, its tree-lined streets, and of course its breathtaking views of the office towers of Wall Street and the historic vistas of the Brooklyn Bridge and the Statue of Liberty.

New York designer Ellie Cullman, of Cullman & Kravis, worked with the owners—the husband a close friend of Ellie's since college—when they first designed the eclectic and sophisticated interiors of their Brooklyn apartment. When they were able to purchase the adjoining one-bedroom apartment, Cullman's clients again called on her and her project manager, Amanda Reynal. "We were so pleased with the previous renovation and redecoration that we hired them again," explains the client.

They trusted Cullman's expertise in redesigning their new master bedroom to take advantage of the additional space now available to them. They wanted to create a room and terrace that

OPPOSITE The view from the hallway outside the dressing room and bath hints of the order and elegance within. The pantry, with a door to the terrace, is visible through the doorway at the opposite end of the room. ABOVE The skyline of lower Manhattan creates a dramatic background for the bustling East River.

would celebrate the stunning vistas of Manhattan and the constant activity on the Hudson River. As the owners say, "We never tire of the view, which is always changing."

The clients' wish list called for shelves to accommodate their diverse book collections, a pantry, a dressing area, a new mantel and marble surround for the fireplace, and a seating area where they could enjoy gazing at the skyline.

Cullman, working with New York architect Scott Kruger, reconfigured the original bedroom to create a dressing room and sitting room for the wife and then converted the newly acquired apartment into a spacious master bedroom with a pantry and a separate dressing room for the husband.

The newly expanded terrace, doubled from its original size, opens off the bedroom and is the perfect spot for family dining, sunbathing, and entertaining. It also offers the ideal perch for watching the myriad activities that New York City is known for, from its world-class sailboat races to its extraordinary Fourth of July fireworks.

The centerpiece of this master suite is a queen-size bed with a beige-fabric-covered headboard and a matching bed skirt, coverlet, linens, and pillows—all from Frette. The

LEFT Extensive collections of books, paintings, nineteenth-century porcelain, and tortoise-shell tea caddies all find a home in this master suite. The triple-glazed walls change color depending on the amount of sunlight spilling in from the terrace. ABOVE A perfect setting for a good book or a romantic meal.

RIGHT *Beach* by Raoul Dufy, 1905, over the mantel. Flower arrangements by Dorothy Waco. BELOW An Anderson & Sheppard of London suit awaits selection of the perfect tie. OPPOSITE A full inventory of clothes and shoes and knowledge about the owner's preference for folded versus hung was necessary before designing this ultimate custom closet. Top shelves provide space for sporting equipment and luggage.

couple's books, their seventeenth- and eighteenth-century Dutch floral plates, and their tortoiseshell tea caddies are housed in built-in bookcases alongside the bed. An upholstered club chair, covered in a tan and ivory chenille, extends an invitation to relax with a good book. "We wanted to create the ultimate master bedroom suite," the designer said.

Cullman knew the importance of outfitting the bedroom with all the necessary lighting for reading, relaxing, or watching television, but she made sure her clients could also adjust the mood with dimmers. The fixtures include Marvin Alexander reproduction brass sconces over the fireplace, contemporary brass pharmacy lamps in the seating area, bookcase lights, adjustable brass lamps above each night table, an early-nineteenth-century twisted-walnut candlestick electrified into a standing lamp, and an Empire-style glass antique chandelier.

Project manager Reynal felt that "the challenge here was to incorporate the new suite's architectural details with the rest of the home while creating a modern, comfortable master suite." It's clear that the Cullman & Kravis solution worked.

TURKISH DELIGHT

estled amid wildflowers in Vermont's Green Mountains, Meadow is one of several cottages designed by Jed Johnson & Associates at Twin Farms in Barnard. A rolling meadow with uncut grass and wildflowers outside welcomes guests into this Moroccan-inspired space.

Built in 1993, the cottage is reminiscent of a desert sheikh's traveling palace. The ceiling has been transformed—with a skilled artisan's brush—to resemble an exotic tent. Floor-to-ceiling brass tent poles of green and gold support the tent, while custom-tile columns in various shades of green, gold, and brown mimic the tent pattern, helping to separate the seating area from the bedchamber. The top of the painted ceiling is gathered at a thirteen-light pierced-tole chandelier that creates a starburst of light.

Intricate patterns and details abound in this Moorish space, from the inlay on the maple desk and the tile work on the chair rail to moucharaby screens surrounding the window. Even the terra-cotta flooring is interspersed with smaller glazed tiles in

ABOVE Elaborate inlay mimics a Turkish rug on this nineteenth-century table set with fresh fruit and wine for the lucky guest. OPPOSITE Rich layering of colors, textiles, wood, and tiles combined with the dramatic effect of architectural details and unusual shapes and patterns culminate in this wildly exotic and tempting space.

OPPOSITE Built-in banquettes flank both sides of the intricate mosaic-tile fireplace. Antique carpets and fabrics were used to create the stunning collection of pillows. FAR LEFT Large windows allow for a view of uncut grass and wildflowers. LEFT An African painted screen. BELOW The armoire conceals a television set.

rich tones of royal blue, red, green, and beige. To soften the tile flooring and to add texture, color, and more pattern to the room the designers layered Moroccan rugs over the bricks.

Guests step down into an exotic bedroom where two nineteenth-century English screens frame the king-size bed. A custom-designed armoire sits between two built-in bookcases and cleverly disguises a television set and extra storage.

A large nineteenth-century Syrian library table serves as a desk, a game table, or a dining table overlooking the blue wildflowers outside. The inglenook fireplace is surrounded by an intricate tile mosaic, while an African stool upholstered in antique leather sits in front of the mantel. Two banquettes covered in a simple John Stefanidis cotton floral print provides intimate seating next to the fire.

The stunning combination of colors, textures, and exotic accessories succeeds absolutely in achieving the Johnson design team's goal to create an exotic and intimate ambience for the fortunate inhabitants of this Vermont getaway.

Architectural Influences

Bruno Romeda — l'Oeuvre

Raj India and the British 1600-1947 · Bayly   NPG

Raj India and the British 1600-1947 · Bayly   NPG

LINEAR CHIC

W ater brings tranquillity," reflects Bob Sweet about his home located on a Connecticut lake. "I love being able to see the water from my bedroom. I find it enormously calming."

Sweet's master bedroom, with its two walls of windows covered by simple string curtains, has an unobstructed view of the water. A terrace outside the bedroom allows him to enjoy the view from outdoors as well. An eastern exposure and a skylight positioned perfectly overhead allow light to flood the space, adding to the drama of this sleek contemporary bedroom.

Architects Warren Arthur and Mai Tsao, who are also Sweet's neighbors and longtime friends, explain their design for this space: "The setting, with its sunrise views and reflected evening light, seemed to capture all the best that nature could give. So, rather than looking inward on itself or suggesting withdrawal from the world, the room seemed to call for an embrace of light and a reaching out to nature."

Sweet observes that he has always used white in his homes'

ABOVE Sliding glass doors onto the deck allow this third-story bedroom to embrace the lake views and capture the best of nature. OPPOSITE The panel behind the Eero Saarinen chair conceals a well-stocked refrigerator. OVERLEAF Color in a white space demands attention.

"The room seemed to call for an

embrace of light and a reaching out to nature.''

interiors. "White is the best backdrop for interesting pieces," says Sweet, "and with white, there is no competition with the art." Paintings by such well-known artists as Marino Marini and James Havard strikingly stand out against the clean white palette Sweet created.

While white is the predominant color in his bedroom, the use of vibrant red is striking. This contrasting color appears in the Eero Saarinen "womb chair" from Knoll, the Mies van der Rohe armchairs, and the Knoll sofa. Smaller accents in red are used throughout the room.

Sweet's bed, a custom design from Manhattan Cabinetry, holds and hides drawers while the clean lines of linen cover the bed. His dressing room was a surprise gift from the architects. According to Sweet, his friends decided to provide him with a place for his extensive wardrobe. Arthur and Tsao designed a long corridor with mirrors and drawers on one side and a hanging wardrobe on the other, to hold clothing, shoes, and linens.

The bookcase nook at the entrance of the dressing room adds texture to the red and white tones of the room. The bookcase is filled with Sweet's collection of books on art and design. He is, he notes, "an avid student of contemporary architecture." And hidden in a corner is a refrigerator stocked for late night snacks and cocktails on the terrace.

Facing the bed and beneath four prints by Marini, a low white custom cabinet holds Sweet's sound system and television set. Speakers are discreetly positioned throughout the bedroom. And on the ceiling, a large mobile echoes the red and black tones of the room as it sways gently with soft breezes from the lake.

SHIPSHAPE

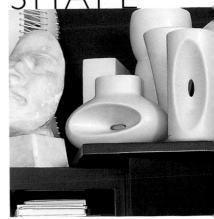

hristopher Coleman lives in a small studio apartment in Midtown Manhattan. With an active design business and social life, he handled the under-500-square-foot space with his busy lifestyle in mind. "Since I am seldom here," he explains, "I wanted to create a hotel-type suite, an all-in-one sleeping, dining, and lounging area complete with a kitchen and bath."

Coleman's advice for other people who live in one-room studios is simple: "Scale, scale, scale! Live with less."

Coleman was impressed by the layout of his small apartment because it had good light and high ceilings. "The place seems spacious to me because of how I placed the furniture, and I deliberately kept the bed, the club chairs, and the ottoman low to accentuate the height of the walls."

Another trick Coleman used to make the room feel bigger was his treatment of the walls. He created bold eighteen-inch-wide

OPPOSITE A satin-lacquer stepped end table from the Christopher Coleman Collection holds an antique African staff and an African horned necklace on a stand. A brown faux fur pillow adds texture and a bit of whimsy to Coleman's sofa bed. ABOVE The grouping of white art pottery and objects on top of an entertainment cabinet from Coleman's collection "started with a simple jug."

stripes using a chocolate brown and cream latex paint. "I did this as an experiment, and it works!"

His daybed, which doubles as a sofa, is from his own furniture collection. He affectionately calls it "the stadium daybed," because he says, "it's low and long and reminds me of a stadium. Its rift oak laminate is a finish used by Jean-Michel Frank in the 1930s and 1940s and one that has regained popularity in the last few years." Coleman began designing furniture because, he says, "I kept noticing missing pieces in the marketplace. I wanted to design such pieces with great style but at a reasonable price."

Cleverly placed in front of the bed is a coffee table he constructed from a console table, which Coleman covered with white leather. The lamp is an old but stylish hospital surgical light he found in a Sag Harbor shop.

For multipurpose storage, Coleman used two cabinets, also from his collection. The maple cabinet holds Coleman's CDs, his bar, and extra linens. The bureau, outfitted with shelves and drawers, holds his clothing.

Coleman chose to hang heavy velvet portiere-style curtains to separate the main room from the kitchen area. "When drawn, these curtains create the feeling that there are more rooms. They also soften the hard edges of all the wood furniture."

In Coleman's own words, the space "screams urban studio," with its sleek geometric lines. He is perfectly content living in this very small space but, like many of us, dreams that one day he will live larger.

ABOVE Dinette chairs from the 1970s are covered in a Donghia stripe. Bolts of fabric from a theatrical supply store are hung on a rod to create a portiere that adds drama and the illusion that another room, rather than a tiny kitchenette, lies beyond. RIGHT Painter's-scrim curtains, bordered with velvet, are simple yet elegant.

ARTS HAVEN

very April a group of talented interior designers put their formidable decorating skills on display at New York's Kips Bay Boys and Girls Club Decorator Showhouse, known to design aficionados simply as "Kips Bay." Working without the impediment of either clients or budget constraints, the designers at Kips Bay use the occasion to produce some brilliant and memorable rooms.

Such was the case with the bedroom that Matthew P. Smyth produced for the 1998 showhouse. "I wanted to create a bedroom that was all-inclusive," he recalls, "a place to read, watch television, write a letter, and have breakfast. A room where you would wake up on a Saturday morning and have no need or desire to leave."

The Smyth bedroom was a rectangular room that contained a central nook with dark turn-of-the-century oak paneling complemented by a rich red fabric from Harry Hinson. As Smyth remarked, "The paneling was dark and heavy. My challenge was to cheer it up with the sisal-colored wool carpet and light fabrics."

ABOVE Detail of objects atop the writing surface and in the pigeonholes of the Georgian bureau bookcase from Florian Papp Antiques. OPPOSITE The juxtaposition of a Kentshire Irish Regency console beneath a contemporary abstract painting in the "foyer" between the bedroom and the bath is stunning. A modern brass table lamp offers a counterbalance to antique English urns.

With a headboard upholstered in biscuit and champagne tones
and white linens embroidered with a beige rope detail, the bed
helped to soften this dark-toned and very masculine room.

Smyth placed a southwestern American Indian mask on
a table beside the bed for its "silhouette and texture." He
says, "I always try to place items that my clients and I find in
our travels. It makes the space more personal."

In one corner of the room is a fireplace with a limestone surround and, in
Smyth's words, "a carved mantel with a
slight Gothic edge to it." A high-back
red wing chair breaks up the area
between the antique Georgian mahogany
bureau bookcase and the fireplace. The
bookcase has a compact writing desk,
and a small leather bench is its companion piece. At the opposite end of the
room, a corner cabinet holds a television
set and stereo system. A Regency console in the entryway is the perfect repository for keys, gloves, and mail. Smyth
added some elegant touches of black: an
English antique urn and a black ceramic bowl holding a fresh
and fragrant bouquet of white roses.

Opposite the bed, Smyth featured one of his designs—a
wood table with a faux granite finish based on a table he
found in Italy. A pair of Regency chairs with their original
leather sit in front of the window and are perfect seats for
enjoying morning coffee and the *New York Times.*

On designing bedrooms, Smyth notes, "A good furniture
plan is essential to start with. Then you can begin to add or
subtract. And I think it's very important to buy the best
linens you can afford. They can make or break a room—not
only for the look, but certainly the feel."

OPPOSITE A cream-
colored bed with white
linens helps to lighten
the dark oak paneling.
A Jean Dubuffet painting
hangs over the bed. Wall
sconces are by Jean
Karajian, based on a
design from the late
1920s. ABOVE Lucite
night tables from the
1960s are an unexpected
but refreshing choice
positioned among
the classic architectural
and fine art elements
in the room.

LEFT Cream-colored curtains and a sisal-colored wool carpet help to brighten the room. TOP A tray designed by Christian Liagre set with an elegant Deco teapot and a curvaceous vase of tulips rests on a table of Smyth's design. ABOVE The fireplace is uniquely placed in the corner of the room. OPPOSITE The painting next to the fireplace is a geometric abstract by Sewell Sillman. The Georgian bookcase is seen here in its splendor, along with an oriental stool.

TUSCAN NUANCE

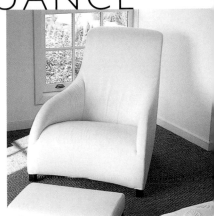

n 1996, Manhattan architect James D'Auria and his actress wife, Jennifer, designed and built a shingled barn-style home in a bucolic setting on the eastern end of Long Island. Here, every weekend for most of the year, they come to recharge and rejuvenate from their busy and engaged lives in Manhattan.

The architecture of the house reflects D'Auria's passion for Italian design and is inspired by the *fienile,* or barns, of the Po Valley, an agricultural sector north of Bologna. "The inspiration came from the *fieniles,*" notes Jennifer, "but James created it in the American vernacular with a modern edge."

Their master bedroom was designed in such a way as to take advantage of the stunning views of surrounding farms and the ocean beyond. "We wanted to wake up to a view of the sunrise, which is spectacular," says Jennifer. "There are windows on three sides, and you are visually thrust out into the fields like a boat on the water, surrounded by nature."

James designed the platform bed of dark wenge wood (a dark

OPPOSITE On the mantel, a photograph by Priscilla Ratazzi depicts Jennifer's footprints in the sand with her dog's beside hers. An Etruscan jug and a sepia print of an ancient pyramid reflect the D'Aurias' love of travel. ABOVE A place in the sun is offered by this modern interpretation of a wing chair from B&B Italia.

LEFT Historical architectural photographs of Florence are lined up over the bed. The telescope is necessary "to see if the surf is strong." Bedside tables are by Italian designer and friend Romeo Sozzi. BELOW The design elements used in the bedroom—sea-grass sisal carpet, dark furniture, and white walls— are repeated in the spacious closets.

oak-looking wood) to be especially low. This allows the couple to take full advantage of the views from the bedroom's three windows; the fireplace, also was designed to be viewed at eye level from the bed.

"The view and the light pretty much determined the layout for the room," reflects Jennifer. "James located the fireplace between two pairs of large windows so that the focus was not split." Notes Jennifer, "We both love the simplicity of white walls and dark furniture. It is very peaceful but at the same time grounding."

Each element in the room complements the house's natural setting. "The window treatments were chosen because of their light-emitting quality; the coverlet and shams because they give a textured relief to the white room." The sea-grass rug adds another texture.

The D'Auria bedroom was thoughtfully designed as a showcase for the unique setting of their house in the picturesque fields of this seaside town. Every element, every shading, and each accessory works to complement the others.

SERENE SANCTUARY

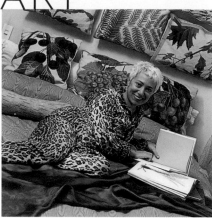

New Yorker Helene Verin lives and works in her 1200-square-foot studio loft in the Flatiron District. A designer of interiors, shoes, and wallpaper, she approached the design of her home with a keen creative eye, turning an industrial loft into a living space that captures her colorful artistic personality.

Formerly the site of a printing factory, the apartment has twelve-foot ceilings and large windows that add to its idiosyncratic charm. Because she operates her business from her home, Verin's challenge was to design not only two bedrooms—one for herself and one for her fifteen-year-old son, Ryder—but also a work area, all without sacrificing her apartment's open quality. As she explains, "I wanted to create a home with privacy for myself and my son, but also retain the feel of a loft space."

For her bedroom she chose to create the feeling of a yurt, or tent, "pitched" within the larger space, to be both calming and enveloping. Verin's philosophy on the renovating process is clear-cut

ABOVE The designer, sporting leopard-print pajamas, does some design research in her favorite workplace, her bed. The botanical-inspired needlepoint pillows, hung as a headboard, are of her design. OPPOSITE Woodgrain prints, especially on fabric, pottery, and other nonwood objects, are Verin's collecting passion. Here, fabric bolsters resemble real logs.

TOP Verin added the leather drawer pulls to the file cabinet, an element borrowed from one of her shoe designs. ABOVE Bookshelves at ceiling height utilize "wasted" space. RIGHT Favorite wardrobe pieces act as artwork in one corner. FAR RIGHT The 1940s Royal Chrome chair holds a pillow designed by Verin. Her son, Ryder, fashioned the hanging lamps from French baking mats.

and direct: "I think great design looks like it's always been there. My apartment is really about me. This is my entire environment, so I needed it to be a serene place, where everything is here for a reason. My apartment became like a piece of sculpture."

She started by designing her bedroom wall on a slant, tent-like, adding frosted-glass panels where light could filter through. She opted for strong color on the wall and painted it "a rich and juicy terra-cotta." Her bedroom "door" is made of linen, which she cleverly strung on wire to create a lightweight portiere.

Verin is an avid collector and designer of textiles, pottery, objets d'art, clothing, wallpaper, and table linens. She likes almost anything with a wood grain, and this passion is indulged throughout her apartment, even down to the duvet pattern on her simple wooden platform bed. Her signature design, which she has incorporated into her headboard, comprises nine botanical-inspired needlepoint pillows she created for the SoHo showroom Michaelian & Kohlberg. Verin took advantage of the room's high ceilings by mounting two walnut bookshelves high up on the wall.

Adjacent to the wall of the bedroom is Verin's closet, which is truly her personal space. "It is a holy place for me," she explains. "This is where I keep some of my most precious things, including my mother's ashes." Verin's closet is expertly organized, creating ample space in which to store all of her clothing and many of her collections, including her trove of vintage clothing and an array of boutique boxes and bags.

As to her sanctuary, Verin says, "I don't need a large space to sleep in. At the end of the day, I love that I can go to my little corner in this big place."

OPPOSITE In the closet, a pony chair atop a wood-grain-print rug. A folded stack of "Jack" fabric by Jack Lenor Larsen sits between vintage luggage. TOP The slanted wall of Verin's bedroom "yurt," as seen from the loft entrance. Opaque glass inserts lighten the space. ABOVE An artfully arranged shelf with a collection of Hermès boxes and an old Schiaparelli compact.

CLASSIC SEASIDE

E very room in the house has a view of either the ocean or the bay," says designer Glenn Gissler of the ten-year-old turn-of-the-century-style house located on a sandy spit on the eastern end of Long Island. Working with a team of architects, Gissler chose not only to give each room access to the bay and ocean vistas but also to connect each to the incredible views.

For the spacious, light-filled master bedroom, Gissler says he wanted to "let the views take center stage." He did this by carefully choosing each piece of furniture, each element. "The dark wood of the bed and the dark-oak paneled floors are in juxtaposition to the translucent shades that filter in the early morning sun glistening off the ocean."

The custom-designed king-size bed, with its mahogany headboard, is positioned to fully enjoy both the ocean breezes and the sunlight flowing in through the ample windows. Doors open to the terrace and sea beyond. The roomy chaise longue at the foot of the bed is "big enough for two people to cuddle," Gissler says.

OPPOSITE The Gothic side chair and the massive bed manage to look crisp and contemporary despite themselves as they stand in sharp contrast to the airy lightness of the room. ABOVE Warm ivory-colored paint on the moldings and mantel are a serene backdrop for the nineteenth-century santos.

The views take center stage in this

Between the chaise and a mahogany-and-rush chair, Gissler has placed a turn-of-the-century French three-tiered table and topped it off with a bit of whimsy: a kaleidoscope from the 1920s and a crystal ball. Beside the chaise, a carved chest holds books and magazines, while underneath, the blue tones in an antique Sultanabad rug pick up similar shades from the sea. "The rug brings some scale to the room," notes Gissler. "We love it because it's simple and very practical."

Above the fireplace, and across the room from the bed a television set situated on a pullout swivel shelf is discreetly hidden behind retractable doors. Gissler and his client wanted the built-in element to utilize the entire wall around the fireplace and to house a high-tech audio and video system.

Gissler feels strongly that bedrooms should be designed and styled to require very little maintenance. "Bedrooms should be easy to live in," and in this seaside retreat, he successfully achieves a "graceful integration" of atmosphere, practicality, technology, and romance.

ABOVE An ebony nursing chair is a sculptural element beside the fireplace. The TV retracts behind a recessed panel. RIGHT French doors open onto the deck and the crash of the surf below. A mix of furniture styles blends into a harmonious whole with the contemporary chaise, the paneled bed, and the Anglo-Indian side tables and chair.

light-filled, serene, easygoing space.

Country Moods

AMERICAN VERNACULAR

Architect Mark Finlay and his wife, Jeanne, renovated a circa 1900 home in Fairfield, Connecticut, for themselves and their four children over a period of seven months. Finlay almost doubled the size of their home by adding to the rear of the house a second entrance, a new kitchen and breakfast area, a family room, a bedroom for their daughter, and a master bedroom suite.

Reflecting on the substantial addition, Finlay recalled, "I drew up the plans in about fifteen minutes. There were lots of restrictions because we live in a historic part of town, so I knew I had to work with the original footprint. I think we really succeeded in keeping the Victorian farmhouse character."

In his busy architectural practice, he notes, "I'm used to making decisions on my clients' behalf. When it's your own house, the decision is more difficult, of course! In this case, Jeanne was not only my wife, but also my client."

And Jeanne knew what she wanted to create. "The downstairs of my home is Victorian country, but I wanted the bedrooms to be

OPPOSITE The delicate lace canopy and earthy soft colors are a dramatic contrast to the dark wood furniture. *The 17th Hole* by Linda Hartough hangs above the mantel. These owners enjoy a roaring fire in the fireplace as often as possible. ABOVE An abundance of pillows makes this bed a comfortable place to work.

more Federal in style, especially because there are so many males in our home, and I think Federal style is more masculine than flowery. My three sons are very comfortable in their own bedrooms, and my husband and I are very comfortable in ours."

To style the interiors, Jeanne started with historical colors from the Federal period. Finlay totally concurred with his wife's choice of the country colors, like the creamy white walls, the dark brown floor, and the sage-green trim. "They are earthy and remind us of our midwestern birthplaces," he said.

For the focal point of their bedroom, Jeanne chose a Shaker reproduction four-poster bed with a hand-tied lace canopy of diamond-patterned linen. The soft green flannel sheets, quilted coverlet, and duvet are complemented by a plentiful collection of pillows.

The Finlays knew they wanted a fireplace in the bedroom. They chose a mantel with details similar to the Victorian style of several pieces they already owned because, said Mark, "it introduced a little bit of detail and mimics some of the detailing of the mirror in the room." Next to the fireplace, a brick-red leather chair is a source of considerable nostalgia for the Finlays—it was the first piece of furniture they bought together for their original home in Fairfield, and it's a favorite place for Jeanne to curl up and read a book, pay bills, or watch television by the flickering light of the fire. "I love winter in our bedroom because of the fireplace," says Jeanne. "I love whatever time I can find for myself there."

Finlay adds, "It's a great old house, and we really use it. Our four kids have lots of friends and pets. This house is lived in, and we love it."

OPPOSITE A wall of cubbies organizes "His" closet, while "Hers" is separate, on the other side of the oak washstand. The molding and the trim are painted in traditional Federal-style colors. The ornately carved Victorian mirror delicately reflects the hand-tied lace canopy. ABOVE Bronze bookends depicting a sleeping infant, circa 1920, support a collection of books.

ANGLER'S RETREAT

There are many very special bedrooms at Twin Farms in Barnard, Vermont, a stylish retreat in the heart of the Green Mountains, where myriad outdoor sports are offered throughout the year. The Perch cottage pays homage to one of them. The interior of this little house celebrates angling, which is, of course, one of Vermont's premier activities, besides skiing.

In 1993 the New York design team of Jed Johnson & Associates designed Perch to be "whimsical and reminiscent of a fishing camp." Named after the freshwater fish, this unique cottage features an extensive and diverse collection of antique fish decoys and carved-fish wall trophies. Antique wooden signs from bait stores and fishmongers line the walls above the banquette; the largest fish—an antique carved painted wood fishing trophy—hangs majestically over the bed in the back of the sleeping alcove.

The cottage, situated above a small stream and beaver pond, is divided into three distinct areas: one for the king-size bed, another for seating and dining, and the third for the desk-cum-

ABOVE An antique partner's desk is placed in front of a panel of mullioned windows overlooking a stone terrace and the pond below. A school of vintage fish signs swim away from the window. OPPOSITE One fish, two fish, old fish, new fish. A ceramic vessel contains wildflowers gathered around the cottage.

LEFT Architectural detail elevates the space, belying the notion of a humble fisherman's cottage. Ample windows allow the room to be bathed in natural light though the cottage is in a wooded setting. Soft earth colors, ambient lamp glow, and a mix of upholstered and wooden pieces create a cozy yet masculine atmosphere.

writing corner. An old-fashioned screened-in porch, a substantial entryway with a "gathering bench," and a large bath with a stylish dressing room complete the spacious layout.

A hand-loomed checkered rug is woven in green and eggshell to complement the ivory walls and sage green trim. The antique mahogany three-quarter-size poster bed fits snugly in its paneled alcove. One member of the Jed Johnson design team recalled: "We liked the niche for the bed because it creates an intimate, warm, and enveloping space." The alcove also cleverly camouflages a television set and ample storage space in a recessed wall cabinet.

A dining table of dark oak is surrounded by antique Windsor chairs. Plump linen pillows and fine cabinetwork line the banquette's two walls, providing guests with comfort for dining, playing games, or reading.

Across from the dining area, a tan love seat and a Victorian tufted chair in a cream-and-green design flank the river-rock fireplace. Above the sofa, an antique screen painted by an unknown artist depicts mountains, water, and trees.

An oversize partners desk is lit by an intricately carved fish-shaped lamp, while two rope-twist stools with wool damask cushions add color and a place to sit—to perch—at the desk.

A fanciful mural of fish, hand-painted by Jim Boyd from Boyd-Reath Studios of New York, leads guests through the dressing room to the bath and beyond. The dressing area, which offers lots of wardrobe space, is filled with natural daylight and a breeze from the adjacent screened-in porch—another welcoming element in this nature-inspired cottage.

ABOVE The entryway contains a built-in armoire and banquette seating—a place to store gear and suit up before wading into the river. LEFT A hallway to the bathroom is fitted with ample storage to unpack clothing and store luggage and extra linens. RIGHT A seating area in front of a large fieldstone fireplace is the perfect spot to open a book and sip a brandy.

ADIRONDACK AMBIENCE

he allure of log cabins is legendary. Dating back to the earliest days of our country, when settlers used timber from the wilderness to build their homes, the first log cabins were usually one-room structures, built of logs laid one upon another, and set with moss, mortar, or mud. Many homeowners today carry on the tradition of building log cabins while adding modern conveniences.

The entrance to the Log Cabin at the Twin Farms Inn in Barnard, Vermont, is a sneak preview of what the design team of Jed Johnson & Associates have in store for guests. Two stone sentinel dogs sit on either side of the hand-hewn-oak nineteenth-century Appalachian homestead, which has been restored as a cabin in the woods. Inside, guests are greeted by a stone wood-burning fireplace and a multitude of canine-inspired objects and paraphernalia. The red gingham curtains, in Cowtan & Tout's Checkers Red fabric, accented with cocker spaniel heads, highlights the room's whimsical dog theme.

This secluded log cabin works well as a multipurpose space

OPPOSITE If this is what it means to be "in the doghouse," then it is a happy condition. The bark-covered log bed is softened with a tufted velvet headboard. Comfortable upholstered pieces make it difficult to keep the dogs off. ABOVE An eerily lifelike Weimaraner appears to have found a hole in the daubing.

RIGHT Adirondack twig chairs pull up to an oak mission-style library table. The adjacent window overlooks the screened-in porch. BELOW Granite slabs top the drawers. A basket contains essentials for the bath. OPPOSITE A hallway fitted with built-in drawers and cupboards doubles as a dressing room. The drawer handles are fashioned to look like dog biscuits. The hand-hooked rug continues the dog motif.

with its four zoned areas: the king-size bed, cozy seating in front of the fireplace, a desk for writing, and a screened-in porch.

The sleeping area sets a relaxed tone for the room with its floral bedspread in dusty reds, deep greens, and browns and its custom-designed Adirondack-style bed made of bark-clad maple boughs. This corner of the room is completed by an eight-star-quilt-covered club chair with dog head finials and a leather trunk intricately decorated with nail heads.

The mission-style oak desk has a built-in bookcase stacked with books wedged between folk art dog bookends. Desk chairs from the Adirondack Furniture Company sit in front of the open Rumford river-rock fireplace with its antique bulldog andirons.

OPPOSITE Dog details even line the mantel and can't help but evoke a smile. LEFT The entrance to the cottage is guarded by two sentry dogs. The snowshoe chair is a Vermont classic. On the entrance table is a magnificent tramp-art clock. Mullioned transom windows on the back wall allow light to spill into the dressing room. BELOW A corner cupboard with more canine collectibles.

An adjacent dressing room complete with several drawers and a wardrobe is not only functional but serves to continue the canine motif. A dressing bench and counter, both of granite, are perfect for holding luggage or clothing, while copper railroad lanterns provide additional lighting.

Many of the dog accessories, from the sculptures and wall hangings to the dog-inspired art, were collected by the owners of Twin Farms—the Twigg-Smith family—from all over this country and from travels in Europe. "Their wish is for many people to enjoy their ever-evolving collection," says the managing director of the inn, Beverley Matthews.

Log Cabin is reminiscent of the cabins that Vermont's early settlers inhabited, but it has been skillfully updated with the luxuries that today's travelers demand.

SEASIDE DREAMS

After years of renting, New York decorator Sarah Smith finally found a property to call her own on the offshore New England island where she and her three children have summered since the kids were small. Smith has renovated her new purchase to allow all of them their own personalized bedroom space and a comfortable home to which they can always return.

Smith was particularly thrilled with her new house because she could finally release from storage the family treasures she had inherited. The centerpiece of her bedroom suite is the heirloom four-poster bed once owned by her great-aunt Vera. "She was probably born in it, and I know she died in it at the age of 108," says Smith. "The bed was turned and carved on the farm in Cedarville, Ohio, where Great-Aunt Vera lived her entire life."

Worthy of the cherished bed are the monogrammed linens custom-embroidered in a blue-and-green vine motif and an organdy overlay by Sethi & Sethi. Other family treasures in the room include a pair of shell-back Victorian chairs, an Edwardian-

ABOVE A nineteenth-century American woolwork pillow is striking against the Colefax & Fowler love seat. OPPOSITE An oil portrait from the 1940s of Smith's mother bathed in sunlight. OVERLEAF A picture window offers a sweeping view of the gardens and the ocean beyond. The door allows barefoot access to the pool.

She could finally release from storage the

family treasures she had inherited.

style writing table, and the portrait in oil of Smith's mother. Her mother also contributed the mahogany chest of drawers, circa 1840, as well as the antique serape rug and the Victorian dresser behind the Dutch door.

Not all of the furniture in the room was passed down through family. The many white-painted cottage-style pieces that Smith has placed in almost every room simply came with the house. "There was a tradition on this island that when a house was sold the furniture was left behind," she explains. "That didn't change until very recently when people started to really decorate their summer houses. Most of the homes here still have these original cottage-style pieces. Keeping this furniture and incorporating it with new upholstered pieces, other antiques, and family heirlooms is part of what makes decorating these houses so much fun."

Smith's room is strategically positioned for garden access and water views. A Dutch door, original to the house, leads to a seating area on the deck. "One of the reasons I bought this house is because of the gardens. The former owner was a landscape designer, and he terraced the yard to allow planting for total privacy around the house and pool," she explains.

A seating area is prettily situated in front of a stunning ocean view. An Edwardian occasional table serves as a coffee table. On the painted side tables, candlestick lamps have custom-made faux tole lampshades with a pierced star design by Dora Helwig.

"When I'm working at my desk I can look out and see the ferry approaching," says Smith. "When it sails to the middle of the picture window, I know it is time to go meet someone coming off the ferry." This makes her window the perfect vantage point for a gracious hostess and a mother whose children make frequent visits home.

OPPOSITE A laptop sits comfortably on the writing table surrounded by fabric, trim, and paper samples—all part of the designer's trade. TOP Family pictures and flowers from the garden on a nineteenth-century mahogany chest. The mirror reflects a Victorian dresser. ABOVE The bed is dressed in linens from John Matouk, a bedskirt from Colefax & Fowler, and an organdy overlay.

BLOOMS OF CHARM

argaret chose this wallpaper for her bedroom because when she first looked at the view outside her window she saw the hillside beyond the pool ablaze with rich pink roses. She wanted to capture that look and feeling for her room," says Sarah Smith, explaining the "Camille" wallpaper from Colefax & Fowler that gives her daughter's bedroom its signature rosy pink glow.

In her island home, Smith has created upper-story rooms for her children and guests by opening up the top floor and tucking bedrooms under the rafters. By converting closets into baths and eking out new closets from under the eaves, she has made delightfully livable spaces from areas traditionally assigned to bats. Each converted bedroom has its own personality.

Margaret's room, like Margaret herself, is a combination of serious and classical, whimsical and fun. The classic elements are the monogrammed Egyptian-cotton linens by John Matouk, the bed skirt and curtains by Brunschwig & Fils, the Osborne & Little trim on the headboard and curtains, and the antique German

OPPOSITE A peek into the room reveals the beaded-board door of the bathroom. The triangular cut in the wallpaper is the only hint that a closet is concealed under the eaves. The antique milk-glass lamp with painted shade is by Dora Helwig. ABOVE Detail of the floor painted by Liz Gourlay and a checked bedskirt.

RIGHT The white-painted furniture is original to the house. John Matouk linens dress the bed. BELOW LEFT A Victorian sewing table does duty bedside. BELOW RIGHT Garden roses in a porcelain pitcher, old books, and a bronze cocker spaniel bookend are elements in a still life. OPPOSITE Monogrammed and embroidered sheets add a personal touch.

milk-glass lamps with gilt paint overlay.

Whimsy comes into play with the lampshades painted to mock the seriousness of the lamps, the decoupaged plates with their rabbit designs, and the floor, painted cottage green with a pink border and a smattering of rose bouquets.

The white-painted Victorian side chairs and the painted cottage dresser with mirror are just plain fun. "They came with the house and here they'll stay," says Smith. They help set the tone for Margaret's carefree, endless-summer bedroom.

ISLAND RESPITE

e is passionate about nature," explains Sarah Smith about her inspiration for the room she designed for her oldest son, Fred, in their island home. "He is studying environmental science in graduate school and is into mountain climbing, hiking, organic gardening, and saving the whales. This room seeks to indulge his passion, albeit in a small way, for the great outdoors."

The painted mural by Liz Gourlay, one of the many artists and craftspeople Smith relies upon in her interior design work, covers the four walls of his room, dramatically reflecting Fred's interest in outdoor life. In muted shades of sage and yellow, blue and brown, the mural depicts eighteenth-century whaling ships, the sailors, and their village—but in this depiction, the whales win! Boats capsize and split in two, spilling sailors into the sea. The whalers all fail to seize their prize.

Although Fred is currently studying in Montana, he is rooted to this island where he spent his childhood summers, and his room

ABOVE An embroidered sheet by Nancy Stanley Waud Fine Linens depicts the central motif of the room. OPPOSITE This small bedroom happily spills out into the garden and the adjacent pool area. The green-painted side table with gilt trim is one of a pair found while antiquing in Hudson, New York.

OPPOSITE A mural by artist Liz Gourlay, in muted shades of sage, yellow, blue, and brown, depicts eighteenth-century whaling scenes. LEFT An antique quilt is mixed with embroidered linens, Ralph Lauren chambray shams, and a vintage cotton blanket with multi-blue stripes for a clean, country look. BELOW Coarse linen Roman shades with deep-sea scallops above as a valance.

pays homage to his eastern seaboard heritage. Atlantic breezes make their way into the room when the door is opened to the garden. Deep-sea scallop shells march around the door and window moldings. On the dresser, an English ironstone platter depicts an American mariner scene.

The bedside lamps, converted from antique stoneware tobacco jars, are a nod to Fred's grandmother in Virginia. The shades were designed with a tobacco-leaf border. The full-size nineteenth-century iron bed is a relic that came with the house. Also indigenous is the painted cottage-style dresser with mirror. Other touches of Americana are the old quilt at the end of the bed and the nineteenth-century fireman's chair. Originally part of a set, the number on the chairback was that of the fireman who sat in that chair.

Smith is justifiably proud of her eldest son and his passion for the natural world. In another bow to his abiding interest, she commissioned Nancy Stanley Waud to design and embroider the whales on the cotton bed linens. "We tease him about saving the whales, but he really is the type that can help make a big difference," says Smith with a smile.

Guest Havens

TELLURIDE NIGHTS

We wanted to make the guest room in our Vermont weekend house a very special place. A guest room in a country house—in my mind, at least—is different from an urban guest room: a bit less utilitarian and definitely a room in which to let your creative juices run free—a space that can transport your visitors to another place and time.

The decor I inherited from the previous owners of our house was charming for its time, but I really wanted to give our guests —in addition to great skiing and snowshoeing and good food and drink—a sense of being someplace very special.

The inspiration for this room, which we fondly call the Telluride Room, began with a roll of wallpaper from Seabrook Wallcoverings, which suggested a log cabin. Our wonderful paperhanger, Mary Farrell, created a look so realistic that many first-time visitors to our home are convinced that we have actually created a true log cabin room within the four walls of our modern mountain home.

OPPOSITE Touching the wall is the only way to convince the eye that the rough-hewn logs and chinking are merely paper. The pecan-colored classic wooden blinds are from Smith & Noble. ABOVE An antique writing table holds books, a candlestick phone, and a leather-bound journal for guests to sign.

ABOVE **A built-in dresser is tucked in next to the closet. One drawer holds extra sheets; the rest are left for guests.** TOP **A basket holds extra guest towels on a faux-antler rack next to the bath.** RIGHT **Two burnished-brass pharmacy lamps provide reading light next to the twin beds. Ralph Lauren floral sheets are an unexpected touch.**

A thick chocolate-colored carpet adds reassuring warmth underfoot, as do the classic wooden shutters, which are reminiscent of earlier times and which echo the wood tones of the wallpaper.

Battered cowboy hats and fedoras, picked up on our travels throughout the Southwest, fill the center back wall between the two twin beds and all are anchored by a deer skull. Thick terry-cloth robes—an inviting touch in any bedroom, hang from an artificial antler rack next to the bathroom door, and vintage black-and-white and sepia photographs of old western and sporting scenes add to the cowboy ambience.

Two black iron beds from IKEA, dressed in cozy red waffle-weave cotton blankets, antique paisley, red gingham, and oversize blue denim pillows, suggest a welcoming and stylish bunk room. Between the two beds sits a plaid love seat that I designed. It is fronted by an antique tavern bench for books and for coffee and cinnamon buns in the morning.

Since this room is not large, every inch of space has been carefully utilized. An antique desk in one corner is stacked with travel books, flowers from the garden, and a compass for long walks. A trunk at the end of one bed is filled with topographical and walking maps, binoculars, and a non-battery Russian flashlight. And nearby stands another of my designs—a comfortable oversize leather wing chair that is an invitation to sit and read, or to close your eyes and take an afternoon snooze.

UNABASHEDLY ENGLISH

Designer Toni Gallagher has designed many bedrooms not only for her clients but also for her family of five. "I try to find what is most pleasing to the eye and what works best for each family, especially my own," she explains.

When Toni and her husband, Jay, renovated their Georgian home several years ago, two bedrooms became one, creating a large new bedroom for their daughter, Jenny. Creating storage space was a primary objective for Gallagher in the renovation. The new room features two entire walls of built-in storage units. One can accommodate a hanging wardrobe and has lots of drawer space for folded clothing. Large cabinets above are perfect for stacking blankets, sweaters, and luggage. The other wall of built-in units features additional cabinets as well as shelves for displaying accessories.

The wall units were chosen, Gallagher recalls, to conceal a chimney and air conditioner, to fill some of the vast space in the large room, and because "they are a great way to keep rooms

ABOVE Jenny's room overlooks the many gardens from which these old-fashioned roses were cut. Silver frames and porcelain boxes create the still life that rests on a nineteenth-century tiered-tole tray table. OPPOSITE The room has the summery feel of an English garden, evoked here by the floral porcelain lamps on a white Scandinavian dresser. A gilded mirror adds a touch of sparkle.

free of clutter. Jenny is delighted with the additional storage space. And with so much room, she doesn't have to switch and store her clothing with the change of the seasons."

Because Jenny's room occasionally functions as a guest bedroom, Gallagher wanted to create a space that would be comfortable and relaxing both for her daughter and for her guests. "My goal was to give it the feel of a retreat," Gallagher says, and with its palette of celadon and cream and its quietly elegant groupings of English antique furniture and accessories, it definitely achieves that goal.

Gallagher enclosed the twin beds within an alcove and framed them with a swag of Colefax & Fowler's Bowood fabric. This print is also used on one of the easy chairs in the room and in Jenny's duvets, shams, bedskirt, wallpaper, and curtains. As a subtle complement to the chintz, Gallagher lined the curtains with an Old World Weavers stripe, which also covers the painted armchairs flanking the upholstered love seat. She purchased the chairs, upholstered benches, and a number of the room's accessories while on one of her many antique-shopping trips abroad. In the seating area, an antique tole tray serves as a coffee table, and a two-tiered table holds her garden roses and family photographs.

A built-in desk area is attractive and handy for Jenny and guests. A desk and an adjoining cabinet holding stationery, CDs, and photographs are thoughtfully placed next to a window with a tree-filled view.

Gallagher says her choice of fabrics is "quintessentially English. Full of personal touches, this is a bedroom my daughter loves coming home to."

LEFT The built-in desk and shelves conceal air-conditioning equipment behind the panels. FAR LEFT Detail of the Colefax & Fowler fabric with matching wallpaper against a painted panel. BELOW Panel doors open to reveal a cedar-lined closet for storing winter woolens, drawers for extra linens and pillows, and shelves for sweaters, handbags, and luggage. OPPOSITE Jenny's growing collection of English porcelain is displayed on the built-in shelves.

"Full of personal touches, this is a bedroom

my daughter loves coming home to."

MAYFLOWER MEMORIES

weekend at one of my favorite getaways, the bucolic Mayflower Inn in Washington, Connecticut, several years ago inspired me to redecorate our guest room at home, a modest-size space that was once the nursery and later the bedroom, replete over the years with teddy bears, trucks, and guitars, of our now twenty-year-old son.

My weekend at the inn reminded me of how much pleasure a comfortable and welcoming guest room can provide. I wanted to provide the same comfort for my guests, who range from my ninety-five-year-old mother-in-law, who travels to us from Boston, to designer friends from California.

A French apple-green desk serves as a night table and writing surface for the mahogany twin beds from the 1940s. On the desk are some of my favorite pieces: two oversize wicker boxes—perfect for storage—a note holder that I picked up on a shopping trip to London, and an antique silver mirror. A soft geometric Axminster carpet is warming even on cold winter mornings.

ABOVE On my own bed, I love piling on the pillows, and I treat my guests to the same. OPPOSITE Colors in this room are subtle and soft, an invitation to our guests to relax. Folding luggage racks are a hotel touch but necessary in this small guest room where storage space is minimal.

LEFT **A desk between the two beds serves as a nightstand for both, though individual Hansen swing-arm lamps offer private reading light. I've provided plenty of writing paraphernalia to promote letters home.** BELOW **A closet is outfitted with guest amenities.**

The walls are covered with my friend Alan Campbell's wide-striped cream-and-white wallpaper—a classic neutral. The coral-patterned curtain fabric is from Colefax & Fowler. This too is a classic, and I love it so much that I had the European shams and the underside of the Frette duvets covered in the same wonderful cotton.

The novels and nonfiction works on the windowsill range from serious political analysis to frothy social commentary to gossipy design tomes. A pair of Hansen swing lamps have practical three-way lighting for night reading.

An enamel-painted breakfast tray can accommodate not only a king-size breakfast with a large cup of latte but also a small bouquet of flowers and the *New York Times.* It is enthusiastically presented each morning to weekend guests.

We had limited closet space in the guest room because I had expanded our master bath several years earlier and in the process had eliminated a portion of an undersize closet. To compensate for the lost storage space I added three new closets on the wall opposite the beds. I keep one closet empty for guests' clothes, and I have outfitted one with the many extras a guest might desire or enjoy—thick terry-cloth towels, extra pillows and blankets, powders, soaps, slippers, and of course a small television set.

CITY SANCTUARY

orking with her bicoastal clients, designer Arlene Pilson completed a major renovation of a two-bedroom Fifth Avenue duplex that commanded striking views of Central Park and the New York skyline. Unfortunately, however, the place had remained essentially untouched since the 1950s. "The apartment was tired," says Pilson. "We gutted it."

Her strategy for the guest room was simple. Since the apartment had only two bedrooms, she decided that one had to function as a combination study and guest room—a place for reading, relaxing, and accommodating overnight guests. "With the addition of mahogany moldings, new mahogany doors, and some good-looking hardware," says Pilson, "we were able to create a sophisticated prewar look in this guest room. We also widened the doorway and installed pocket doors. Now, since it's so close to the master bedroom, it feels like a suite."

One vital acquisition for this room was the sleeper sofa. Pilson wanted one that looked like a traditional sofa but was as roomy

OPPOSITE Wool billiard cloth tacked to the wall provides a strong graphic element and an extra sound barrier against the traffic of Fifth Avenue below. The open door leads to a full bath. ABOVE A view of the closet, which has a pull-out laundry bin, cubbies for storage, and a tie rack, all with ample lighting.

and comfortable as a standard bed. Fortunately, John Rosselli had a custom-made sleeper sofa that answered all these requirements. Pilson was delighted with his design: "It has luxurious down feather cushions and a very relaxing inner-spring mattress, with an easy-to-use opening mechanism."

The designer also wanted to make the room serene, enveloping, and quiet, so she upholstered all four walls with a wine-colored billiard cloth that is a mixture of wool and nylon. The rug—a handmade floral design from Pakistan in burgundy, rose, and greens—inspired her choice of the bur-gundy wool blend on the walls. "It took the workmen a month to pound in all the nailheads to finish off the uphol-stered walls. We had to do the math and figure out the grid to make every nail fit in perfectly."

Pilson has done many projects for this couple. "I've been fortunate enough to be a part of the selection process for all of their homes," she says. "The previous two projects are very contemporary, but they wanted this New York City apartment to have a warm traditional feel. The common denominator in all three spaces is a spectacular view!"

LITERARY LICENSE

"T his room is a mirror of my life and travels all over the world," reflects designer Stephanie Stokes on the guest room in her Manhattan apartment. "I could have done this room in traditional Upper East Side good taste," she goes on. "But you know what? It would have been quite boring! This room is really my world and reflects my friendships and travels."

The elegant space is effortlessly multifunctional as library, guest room, media room, home office, and bar. Stokes's design for the room was inspired by the eighteenth-century English architect, Sir John Soane, who is credited with introducing the romantic, yet stylishly eclectic look to British design.

"The room is a mixture of patterns," she says, "Turkish fabrics, Afghan benches, African pillows, contemporary English botanical drawings, Moroccan tables, a pair of Louis XVI chairs, and a world-class English Regency desk." The guest bed is a sleeper sofa covered in a fabric designed by Sally Metcalf for Christopher Norman, Inc. Its lush pillows do double duty when the sofa

ABOVE Stokes thoughtfully provides guests with notebooks full of advice, from where to get the best take-out to what to do in an emergency, say, if the ice maker breaks down. OPPOSITE All the cozy luxury of sleeping in a library—rich volumes of reading material, warm wood paneling, and golden light.

LEFT The doorway on the left leads to the bathroom. Paneled built-ins conceal entertainment technology, guest linens and pillows, and hanging closet space. A window banquette provides additional seating and an out-of-the-way spot for an extra phone and a laptop. BELOW Old photograph albums are fun to pore over on a chilly autumn day.

becomes a bed, providing support behind the white and salmon-pink sleeping pillows.

Stokes enjoys playing hostess. "I love having friends visit from all over the world. It's my way to return the hospitality I've been given," she says.

Much of the room is lined with floor-to-ceiling bookshelves, filled with favorite novels as well as books written by Stokes's friends. Recessed shelves hold treasures that she has collected on her travels. The color of the striated blue-green paint, she says, is from her memory of the fourteenth-century tapestries in the Cluny Museum.

The well-stocked bar, located near the entrance to the guest room—and the apartment—is perfectly positioned for welcoming cocktail hour guests. The bar's unique wall covering is made of leather book spines glued to the wall; Stokes had it custom-made in England. Glasses are hidden behind cabinet doors.

Stokes has left no detail unattended to. "I'm very aware that today's houseguests have specific needs," she says. "I have a laptop, a fax machine, and a separate, private phone line with its own answering service. With guests from around the world, the separate phone line keeps us sane."

Elegantly unique storage solutions are

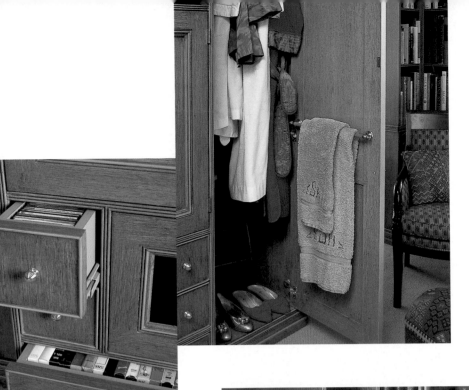

LEFT A brass bar inside the closet is hung with monogrammed towels. A selection of terry cloth and silk robes ensures that guests won't struggle with "one size fits all." BELOW Multitasking is taken to new levels when one can mix a drink and send a fax at the same time. Bar glasses are hidden behind paneled doors—the panels being a mosaic of leather book bindings.

OPPOSITE The entryway of Stokes's apartment, with library access behind the paneled door. The rest of the apartment gets all the natural sunlight that the library is denied. Stokes made this negative a positive by deliberately making this room a dark, cozy space. ABOVE Drawers expressly designed for video and CD storage.

a Stephanie Stokes trademark.

PRETTY IN PINK

love saturated pinks!" muses Jamie Drake. "I think people look fabulous in pink interiors. Pink is especially flattering in bedrooms, and it is always a pleasant surprise for my guests!"

Drake chose a tulip pink for the guest room in his Long Island, New York, home because, he says, "I wanted a bright color, since it's truly a fantasy room." One weekend guest at the noted designer's home described looking into the pink bedroom as like "gazing into a seashell. As the light changes in the room, the pink on the wall subtly changes."

The focal point of this space is the bed with its headboard upholstered in a vintage fabric from Decorators Walk and accented with a satin rope trim in shades of pink. Drake says he favors padded headboards for the sheer comfort they lend to sitting up in bed. A dog-friendly charcoal-gray blanket covers the crisp white sheets, and a floral-print comforter is draped across the foot of the bed. The tailored white shams are bordered in sherbet pink and stacked behind iridescent and beaded pillows.

OPPOSITE Translucent turquoise and a blue-glazed jug become exciting color punches in this pink-hued room. Snapdragons and delphiniums were cut from Drake's gardens. ABOVE An old country dresser with original paint is a fun find, even more so because the original owner liked pink as much as Drake does.

As the light changes, it is like gazing

Indonesian mahogany side tables are paired with a late-nineteenth-century country dresser—worn but still sturdy—that can accommodate weekend wardrobes for guests. Notes the ever-thoughtful Drake: "I always outfit every guest room with slippers, bathrobes, television set, VCR, and telephone."

What he calls a "screwy-Louis French-style chair" has been transformed into something more casual by stripping the paint and covering it in a woven straw cloth, to give a decidedly countrified twist, belying its origins. Next to it, a French bistro table with a vibrant blue glass top and a vase of fresh flowers from Drake's garden make visitors feel well taken care of.

This special guest room is a splendid repository for the finds from Drake's countless forays into flea markets and antique shops throughout the world: a nineteenth-century French ashtray, porcelain shells glazed in the palest tinge of pink, and a watercolor by the society artist Emlen Etting. Each detail adds panache to a place where pampered guests not only relax within, but also gaze out at the picturesque gardens and the sparkling blue pool below.

ABOVE A mahogany-stained floor and the round bedside tables are the only dark elements in this ethereal room. RIGHT Because of the play of light on the slanting walls, the room looks as if it is painted in multiple shades of pink rather than one solid color. The pillows on the bed mimic the colors in the floral bouquet.

into a shell with evolving pink hues.

CHENILLE FANTASY

The Anchorage is one of the earliest summer residences on an island off the New England coast. The island had been populated since before the Revolutionary War by fishermen, farmers, and other year-round residents, but building a grand house to be used exclusively for summer living was a more recent nineteenth-century notion.

Although the three-story gabled structure has been extensively renovated, the charm of the original does not fade. The third-floor guest room, in particular, retains a nineteenth-century charm and simplicity that bespeak the sunny, airy delights of summer.

"The white-painted cottage furniture and iron beds in this room are original to the house," remarks Sarah Smith, a New York City interior designer who has employed a restrained hand at the Anchorage for her clients, a couple from Maryland. "Even the little slipper chair is original, though we had it covered in a Scala-mandre fabric. That was the fun of working in this house. The owners loved the original furnishings, and so we just selected

ABOVE A charming mix of old-fashioned textiles. OPPOSITE Simple pleated shades are the only window treatment in this sunny aerie. Cleverly deceitful, the rose in the bud vase will never lose its bloom—it is artfully crafted of silk and stuck in acrylic, leaving the watering can free to fulfill its destiny as a lamp.

LEFT The mellow blue and white is given a punch with bouquets of the owner's prized dahlias, which she generously bestows around the house. ABOVE A Victorian bamboo étagère holds reading material bedside.

fresh cottons, linens, and chenille to bring them up to date but to keep that carefree summer feeling."

Simplicity is key, but whimsy rescues the room from starkness. An Osborne & Little wallpaper titled "Beneath the Waves" suggests a seaside grace. In the design, sea horses and stars float in the current of a pale blue field. Old-fashioned white chenille bedspreads and pillow shams are from Chelsea Editions. The cottage look resonates in the muted blue and multi-toned rag rug, the blue-and-white antique quilt, and the bedside lamp made from an old watering can. The only vibrant colors are provided by flowers from the garden and by the pink of the sunset.

The mood of an earlier time is reinforced by the absence of technology—in this room, reading, relaxing, and day-dreaming are still preferred. With a chair next to it for comfortable gazing, the third-story window offers a lovely view of the gardens, the Anchorage dock, and the sunset over the water.

Children's Hour

LOFTY SLUMBERS

Penny Drue Baird is a New York—based designer who lives in a brownstone house on the city's East Side with her husband and family, including two young sons, Benjamin and Philip.

Baird is an expert designer of children's rooms, having created rooms for her six sons (and stepsons) over the last twenty years in addition to projects she has completed for clients.

For seven-year-old Benjamin, Baird has created a warm and cozy bedroom, most notable for the bed, which sits in a niche atop ample drawer storage. Young Benjamin scrambles up a library ladder to his bed, where he can close the Old World Weavers wool plaid curtain to create a tent-like effect. As Baird remembers, "When I was small, I loved having my bed in a cubby. It was very cozy." The bed's headboard is a bookshelf, which Benjamin has filled with Beanie Babies. The end of the bed holds some of his favorite toys and stuffed animals.

A sensible designer, Baird loves to find or create pieces that do double duty. An antique bench also serves as a toy chest and can

ABOVE A collection of globes reflects a love of travel and a curiosity about the world. Travers wallpaper casts a warm glow in this idyllic boy's room. OPPOSITE Surrounded by soft stuffed animals and with curtains around his cubby bed, Benjamin has the perfect spot to retreat and enter his imaginary world.

"When I was small, I loved

easily "stow his costumes—we are a big Halloween family," Baird says. It sits between two large windows framed by blue cotton panels with a whimsical animal print. An English leather and mahogany bureau provides additional storage space and is topped with Benjamin's collection of globes, while a desk with a hanging cupboard above it neatly hides books, videos, and autographs of sports figures.

Baird enjoyed creating her son's room, which she describes as "cozy, warm and happy." About the eclectic pieces in the room, she explains that the decision to use or not use antique furniture depends on the child. "Fabrics that are luxurious must also be durable," she says. "Fragile fabrics can be reserved for windows."

Benjamin is thoroughly pleased with his bedroom. "I think my room is a nice place to be," he says. "The drawers under my bed are cool, and there's also a bed for my friends to sleep over. I also like my desk 'cause it used to be my mom's."

having my bed in a cubby. It was very cozy."

FAR LEFT Detail of bed curtains. The wool plaid is "Macmillan" from Old World Weavers, set off by the sisal rope tiebacks. LEFT Detail of the desktop. An antique blotter with rock samples and a paperweight. The diorama in a shoe box is a Benjamin creation. Colored twig pencils are as fun to look at as they are to use.

RIGHT Stuffed animals reside with a collection of Halloween costumes in this antique toy bench. The cotton curtain fabric depicts Victorian animal prints in ornate frames. It is repeated in a cushion on the toy bench. OPPOSITE Benjamin inherited an impressive collection of sports memorabilia from his older brothers, who are now in college. An antique cupboard contains that collection and more.

L'ENFANT

hen Penny Drue Baird, of the New York design firm Dessins, designed the nursery for her youngest son, Philip, she had a definite idea of what she wanted to achieve in this very personal project in her own home.

"I wanted to create a nursery for Philip that was as soft and cozy as any fairy tale could be," she says. "Since he was my last baby, I wanted my every fantasy about babyhood to be expressed. My first baby had slept in the kitchen! I am close to my boys, and we spend a lot of time in their rooms."

Baird's cerulean blue nursery is a large room on the third floor of a New York City town house and features many of the wonderful details often found in these architecturally distinguished houses—unique moldings, a fireplace, wonderfully aged wooden floors, and windows rising to the generously high ceiling.

Baird designed two armoires with pullout wicker baskets underneath for use as storage space for clothing, books, toys, blankets, and other essentials. One even features a pullout dressing table.

OPPOSITE The armoire, perfectly outfitted for a baby's needs, will easily adapt for an older child. The changing table becomes a desk while the shelves adjust for bigger clothes and books. ABOVE Detail of upholstered door, cleverly piped around the edges and doorknob. "Thank Heaven for Little Boys," indeed!

TOP On a round table, a burlap tablecloth with blue overlay cleverly conceals baskets of baby books and toys. ABOVE Treasures of childhood amassed on the mantel— silver spoons, teething rings and cups, a Limoges box for *"dents de lait,"* and a Halcyon Days enamel collection. RIGHT Child-size and adult furniture, including a pull-out love seat, means everyone is comfortable spending time in the nursery.

The crib is painted white and of a classic design complete with soft white cotton Pratesi sheets with blue ostrich designs. Next to the crib, a table draped in blue fabric holds children's books, a basket of audiotapes (some in French since Philip is growing up with both languages), and a small lamp with a pierced-paper shade.

The walls are covered with a blue check taffeta from Christopher Norman. "I upholstered them," says Baird, "because it softens sound and creates a soft and luxurious feeling."

Baird designed the window treatments using a reverse box pleat valance trimmed with small plush bunnies. A blue checked fabric paired with a custom-designed matelassé fabric embossed with the ABCs completes the luxurious layered look.

Between the tall windows is a blue polka-dot convertible sofa bed, a snug place for Baird and Philip to read a book. Across the sofa lies a cashmere-and-wool blanket embroidered with the word *"Bébé."* A small chair covered in matelassé toile de Jouy sits by the crib with one of Philip's many stuffed bears.

The marble fireplace mantel is the stage for a collection of enamel Battersea Christmas boxes and cherished silver baby cups, rattles, and hairbrushes.

A resourceful touch to Philip's room is the upholstered "hidden door" leading to his parents' bath. About the second entrance, Baird says simply, "It makes it easier to give the baby a bath, and I'm just a few steps away."

Baird has filled Philip's room with soft fabrics and soothing colors to create a nursery that she says, "looks like childhood should feel."

OPPOSITE A sleepy bear catches the last rays of the day in a plush crib dressed in Pratesi linens. ABOVE Clown dolls lazily swing in the windows while little bears happily add trim to the reverse box pleats in the valence. A sisal-colored wool rug is durable yet comfortable under foot and bottom.

NANTUCKET REVISITED

ine-year-old Spencer has spent his summers on the island of Nantucket with his parents and sister. Happily, at a very young age he fell in love with the sea and all things nautical. It was only logical, then, to design his bedroom around his passion.

"Parents sometimes have a hard time deciding how to design a child's room," observes Spencer's mother, designer Cindy Rinfret. What she recommends, and what she has done with her own son's room, is to design it around the child's particular interests, keeping in mind how these rooms can grow with your child.

Spencer's bedroom in a southern Connecticut suburb is filled with furniture and nautical accessories that reflect his youthful enthusiasm and create a comfortable and colorful backdrop for his room. One of his favorite pieces is his unique bookshelf, which has been crafted out of an old wooden rowboat. On an adjacent bookshelf, Spencer has arranged vignettes of his treasured collection of bottled ships, a shadow box filled with nautical rope knots, and his three beloved teddy bears, which "he

OPPOSITE "The sailor's life is the life for me," the theme of Admiral Stebbins's room, is appropriate for a child who learned to walk and talk on Nantucket. The headboard is an English antique, found in disrepair and resurrected by an artist with an eye for the sea. ABOVE Bears and boats atop a bookcase.

carried with him everywhere in his early years," Rinfret says.

Spencer is especially proud of his bed, with its hand-painted headboard naming him Admiral Sir Spencer Stebbins. A fire-engine-red Ralph Lauren duvet cover and pillowcases, nautical blue-and-white-striped sheets, and a blue European sham adorn his bed. A creamy fabric with a blue sailor's-rope motif from Colefax & Fowler is used for the bed skirt and window treatments. An assortment of America's Cup winning sailboat prints line the walls above his bed.

At the foot of his bed, a toy chest with rope handles has a canvas-upholstered seat painted as a treasure map, providing extra storage and a resting spot for "Tony Orlando," a large stuffed toy turtle that Spencer found in Florida.

The color of the walls sets the palette for the rest of the room. Rinfret chose a marine-blue paint, striated and glazed above the chair rail, which is stained mahogany to match Spencer's rowboat bookshelf. She anchored it with a white beaded board wainscoting beneath.

The dresser was custom-painted by a Nantucket artist with a scene from one of Spencer's favorite places—the Brant Point Lighthouse. Above it hangs *Reaching for Nantucket* by Michael Keane, the well-known painter of nautical scenes. And in a place of honor is a mounted trout, the largest caught at the Ausable Club in the Adirondack Mountains in 1996. Spencer reeled in that trout at the tender age of four, with a little help from his father.

Personal touches are important to his mother, who has strategically placed framed family photos around the room. "I think it's important that children remember the fun times spent with friends and family—to be able to wake up and fall asleep feeling secure and loved."

TOP Spencer wakes up each morning facing this view of the Brant Point Lighthouse on his dresser. Historic boat reliefs hang on the left. ABOVE Round side tables, supported by iron-and-tin racing flags, are topped by brass lanterns by Ankerlight. OPPOSITE Spencer leads a ship-shape life, with his clothes laid out and ready for school and his bookbag packed.

BALLET DREAMS

W ith two children of her own and a growing clientele of parents who seek her guidance in decorating their children's spaces, interior designer and shop owner Cindy Rinfret loves the challenge of working with these rooms. She attributes the strong interest in children's rooms to the increase in larger families among her clients and their sophisticated design sensibilities. "Today, many affluent families that I know are having more children. So it makes sense for them to design rooms that their children can grow with."

In decorating a room for her seven-year-old daughter, Taylor, Rinfret chose furniture, objects, and colors that would nurture her daughter's imagination and love of dressing up. She says, "I wanted Taylor's room to be like stepping into a sweet dreamland. Her favorite colors are pale blue and pink, and we wanted to work with that palette in the room."

The setting for Taylor's dreamland is the mural created by set designer John Pascoe, which he hand-painted on the three walls,

ABOVE The Victorian dollhouse is actually a storage cabinet containing a collection of head bands and hair ribbons. OPPOSITE Taylor, dressed in one of her play outfits, snuggles with her beloved stuffed mouse. OVERLEAF A four-poster bed and a theatrical mural set the stage for a little girl's dream room.

"I wanted Taylor's room to be like

stepping into a dreamland."

RIGHT A reproduction Staffordshire figurine lamp beside the bed. FAR RIGHT The Victorian house in the mural mirrors the storage cupboard on Taylor's dresser. Furniture is scaled down to her size.

ABOVE Mirrored closet doors are perfect for "dress-up" parties and reflect the mural fantasy in mullioned splendor. OPPOSITE Taylor's room is designed with plenty of room for her to grow. Now half of her plentiful closet space is filled with pink costumes, but the teenage Taylor will find plenty of use for the extra space.

and accentuated with the fourth wall's mirrored closets. The mirrors are perfect for adding sparkle, for playing dress-up, and for getting ready for school. The small coat rack, personalized with Taylor's name, holds one of her favorite costumes—her sequined pink tulle ballet tutu.

With suggestions from Rinfret, Pascoe created a "dreamlike backdrop," says Rinfret, "that is like a luscious romp through a cloud-filled landscape." Much of the design was inspired by Rinfret's own fondness for English gardens. "I love them because there is always a surprise to be found, something unexpected." Architectural details—trellises, a pagoda, birdhouses, even a dollhouse inspired by Taylor's own dollhouse—birds, and monkeys are featured in the scene.

Rinfret says Taylor looks forward to the day when her hand-painted twin-size bed will be covered with a canopy—a change her mother will make to further enhance this special room.

VICTORIAN CHILDHOOD

bedroom that is designed around a love for horses and bears—that's the space designer Danielle Austin created for ten-year-old Laura Furey.

Laura's enthusiasm for horses comes from a long family tradition. Both of her parents ride, and her grandfather is still an active competitive rider. She adores riding with him during visits each spring and summer in Virginia. Laura's mother, Julie, sparked her daughter's interest in stuffed bears when she passed down her own collection to her only child. As Julie remarks, "We love poking through shops looking for bears to add to her collection."

In all children's rooms, the challenge parents and designers face is how to balance a young person's paraphernalia and gear with a need for order and organization, while at the same time teaching children the value of cleanliness. Laura's room was no exception.

An oversize Swedish Blond armoire with antique lace curtains behind the lattice door panels was the perfect solution for her particular needs. Painted yellow and strategically placed in

OPPOSITE A Victorian teddy, dressed for an outing, perches on the nightstand. ABOVE Swedish country–style dresser and bed will carry Laura through to her teens, while a well-organized armoire is a perfect storage solution for a child of any age. Botanical prints and English porcelain plates add a romantic touch.

"It gives me great pleasure to see their

the room, the armoire houses a television set, Laura's bears, a wooden pole on which to hang the bears' clothes, and plenty of sheets, blankets, and towels for girlfriend sleepovers. Explains her mom, "Kids' toys come in odd shapes, and the armoire's height and depth work well to hold most of Laura's playthings." An antique walnut toy chest with detailed carvings provides extra storage. On top of it sit more of Laura's favorite teddy bears.

"The fabric I chose," Austin explains, "is a cheerful, crisp floral print that uses the blue, white, and yellow color palette Laura wanted to incorporate in the room. The room is not large, so I wanted to keep the color palette as consistent as possible to give it a greater sense of spaciousness."

Laura's bed creates an atmosphere of femininity with its rosette crown canopy of delicate lace. It is complemented by balloon-shaded windows in the same floral fabric used on the pillow shams and on an upholstered club chair in the corner.

Austin enjoyed designing Laura's room. "Children's rooms let me stretch my imagination a little further because they allow me to be more whimsical," she says. "The kids I have worked with all seem to have definite ideas about what they want in their rooms, and it always gives me great pleasure to see their faces as I help create their space."

RIGHT A Victorian pull-toy horse with original hair bespeaks Laura's love of horses. She found it in an antiques store while shopping with her mother. Under the window, the antique toy chest and rocker invite Laura to read a book or talk to her bears. Grown-up-size chairs patiently await her.

faces as I help create their space."

GARRET HIDEAWAY

When we moved from Manhattan to our home in Westchester County almost twenty years ago, our sprawling, century-old Norman-style stucco house had two garret-type attic rooms. One became the au pair's room when our children were young; I turned the other into a home office where I would escape to work on my books and other design projects.

Today these two spaces—made much more comfortable with some creative reconfiguring over the years—are the bedrooms of our two sons, college-age Patrick, and Nick, who's still in high school. Nick's room is fairly narrow, with sloping walls that follow the roof lines of the house. To admit light and summertime breezes, several years ago we inserted two skylights. At the same time, we had our contractor, Zoltan Horvath, create a built-in niche over the head of the bed to house Nick's growing collection of sports trophies and collectibles and to accommodate his passion for anything related to his beloved New York Yankees.

ABOVE Nick, with frequent visitors Lola and Winnie, sprawls out in his well-made bed. OPPOSITE Besides doing an incredible job horizontally hanging the wallpaper, once again our intrepid paperhanger, Mary Farrell, cleverly disguised the actual chimney casing with a fieldstone-print wallpaper and then faux-painted the roof beams to resemble granite slabs. Corduroy valances disguise inexpensive window shades.

OPPOSITE With the garret's propensity for chill, piles of blankets and comforters ensure that Nick stays toasty warm. RIGHT Boxes and drawers help keep Nick's stuff organized—no easy task. MIDDLE This low-to-the-ground chair works well with the sloping ceiling. BOTTOM A chair for guitar practice and shelves for books and stereo equipment.

About a year ago a wonderfully imaginative and authentic-looking log cabin wallpaper pattern, created by Seabrook, captured my attention and inspired me to do a makeover of Nick's room. With the help of my talented wallpaper hanger, Mary Farrell, I was able to transform the room into a cozy and rustic hideaway. It's a great room for a teenage boy and, for Nick, a welcome change from the more formal decor of the rest of the house.

I found a black iron bed for Nick's room that nicely complements the bunkhouse ambience. Red flannel sheets and shams from Ralph Lauren work well with a solid red fleece throw and a tartan plaid cotton and velvet patchwork quilt. A framed rodeo poster by Fritz Schoelder hangs over the bed.

A simple blond oak desk provides a work space for studying, while a durable fire-engine-red chair is perfect for reading either *Macbeth* or *Sports Illustrated.* The low-slung chests of drawers work perfectly under the sloped walls to offer maximum storage and to serve as a showcase for Nick's collection of autographed sports books and other memorabilia.

The log cabin wallpaper is certainly the defining element in Nick's room, creating a backdrop for what had been an awkward space. And it is timeless—not just suitable for a young boy but also appropriate for a teenager.

MIA'S ROOM

Before Mia and her family moved from Des Moines, Iowa, to Rye, New York, four years ago, she had her own room with a double bed, a built-in headboard, bookcases, and a built-in dresser in a walk-in closet. So it was quite a change for Mia, now fourteen, to move into a smaller house, to have no furniture of her own, and to suddenly have to share a room with her six-year-old sister.

The room assigned to Mia and Claire was a converted attic. While large in floor space, slanted ceilings reduced its headroom, and only small pieces of furniture could be maneuvered up the attic steps. A poorly conceived earlier renovation had made the walls appear to be sagging, and the floor was covered with a white carpet that quickly became stained with cocoa, nail polish, and felt-tip pen markings. "I was stuck with Claire and all her little toys, a twin bed, and no space at all for any of my own stuff," recalls Mia.

The situation could not last. After renovations in the Rye house, the girls' parents were able to move Claire into her own

OPPOSITE A cushion in a sunny window seat is covered with a vintage quilt. Mia, a budding artist, stores paints underneath. The pillow cover in the wicker chair is made from an old feed sack given to her by her great-grandfather in Iowa, whipstitched around the edges. ABOVE Mia with her cat, Charlie.

LEFT Mismatched twin beds, one from
a thrift shop and the other passed down
from Mia's mother, coexist peacefully
when dressed in matching bedding.
Outgrown children's furniture from an old
Sunday-school classroom is now used
as a bedside table and a nightstand. Painted
multiple times, it remains serviceable.
The curtain rod is a curbside treasure.

room downstairs, and Mia was free to claim the attic and make it hers. Fortunately for the teenager, the space came with its own full bath.

Mia had very definite ideas about the look of her room. She wanted it to be reminiscent of the summer cottage she visited each year on an island in Maine. She chose wainscoting and paint the color of beach sand. Mia asked for an enamel-painted floor so it would feel like a boat deck under her bare feet, but when the rug was discarded, it became clear that the flooring underneath needed to be replaced. Mia and her mother chose a whitewashed laminate to look like wood and to lend the space an airy summer feel.

"She was limited with furniture," explains her mother. "We kept the twin beds up there, but we could only get one small dresser up the stairs. We decided to have our contractor, Scott Simonsen, construct a built-in bookcase. While Mia can store clothes and books on the shelf now, I have in mind that when she goes to college this room may become my office."

Scott also added a window seat and shelves to house Mia's videotapes, books, and collectibles. An antique French drop-leaf table serves as a desk.

"I love my room now!" exclaims Mia. "It is easy to keep neat and organized, and because it is so sunny up here, this is where Charlie and Emma [the family cats] also like to hang out.

"Now," she says, "if I only had a piano, a small refrigerator, and a microwave, I wouldn't even have to come downstairs on weekends."

"She won't get that," says her mother, laughing. "Now that she has her own room, we don't see enough of her as it is."

Nature's Way

MOUNTAIN BREEZES

Vermont in the summer is notable for a multitude of dazzling attributes—lush green meadows and mountains, sparkling blue streams and lakes, charming country inns, and much more. One of my favorite Vermont summer features is its warm days and cool evenings, so inviting for outdoor living.

Summer porches are the romantic staple of many lakeside and seaside cottages in New England. Luckily our thirty-year-old house in Vermont has an old-fashioned summer porch, generous in size with its cedar beams and a whirling fan overhead. The previous owners, who worked with the architect and builder of the house, the late and talented Bud Lench, had added a nifty touch by installing translucent bronze-colored shades that are fabulous for darkening the porch for a lazy afternoon nap.

When my sister Jeanne visited me this summer from her home in France, I decided, on an impulse, to use the porch as her bedroom. She absolutely adored her fresh-air experience, and I have the feeling that it will become a tradition, not only for her, but for

ABOVE A sponge bath is a delicious awakening with soap in a milk-glass dish and warm water in an enamel bucket. OPPOSITE Mosquito netting is graceful, ethereal, and practical. Once the bed was made, this room was set up in minutes—all the furniture is lightweight and portable and moves easily indoors and out.

BELOW A retrofitted picnic basket stored under the Parsons "dressing" table includes robe and slippers, toothbrush and paste, towels and a washcloth. RIGHT A telescope, borrowed from the living room, is focused on the adjacent mountain ridge. Winnie loves our Crate & Barrel butterfly chair. A fan encourages the breeze.

many of our other summer guests.

I set up in one corner of the porch a rustic twin-size log bed under some white gauze mosquito net hung from the porch rafters. Crisp cotton bedding topped with a well-worn vintage matelassé coverlet adds to the *Out of Africa* ambience that the decor suggests. A Parsons table covered with a white linen tablecloth serves as an intimate dressing table that is perfect for holding bath paraphernalia as well as a practical chrome mirror. The bedside table, which in actuality is a galvanized-steel butler's table, provides just the right modern touch, and glass and linen lamps are perfect for nighttime reading under the covers. A simple canvas butterfly chair sits next to the dressing table, and another is placed next to the bed.

Selective accessories complete this summertime tableau: a vintage reproduction fan, a bronze telescope, and, under the Parsons table, an old-fashioned picnic basket transformed into a basic overnight kit for guests. The kit holds such necessities as towels, toiletries, and fresh toothbrushes.

This very special summer space was easy to create and fun to spend the night in. What could be better than retiring to the cooling New England evening breezes with a good book and the sounds of Vermont Public Radio and the crickets in the background?

HOSPITABLY BIRCH

ith its vaulted ceiling of Adirondack twig work, Treehouse at Twin Farms Inn in Barnard, Vermont, does indeed give guests the sensation of being in a very relaxed, stylish room in the treetops. The cottage was designed in 1993 by the New York firm of Jed Johnson & Associates.

A birch bark motif, reflecting the Vermont milieu, permeates the space. The woolen rug has birch bark coloration and works well with a sophisticated toile fabric in a soft black, gray, and cream. Handcrafted by the noted artisan Daniel Mack, birch log trellises frame the windows, serving as natural valances, and toile curtains are dressed with diamond-scalloped fabric valances, edged in red rickrack and topped off with wooden acorn tassels.

The nineteenth-century four-poster bed has been stained a blackish brown with a wax finish. Perched ravens—the finials on the barley-twist bedposts—echo the treetop theme, and an oversize antique trunk at the foot of the bed is draped with a

OPPOSITE Incredible craftsmanship is displayed everywhere in this room, whether in the birch-bark-veneer bookcases with natural twig end panels or in the Japanese stoneware jug and lacquered red box. ABOVE On the screened porch, a birch-twig rocker with woven back and seat commands a bird's-eye view of the surrounding woods. A gurgling brook provides background music.

A birch bark motif, reflecting

the Vermont milieu, permeates the space.

geometric-patterned quilt. An antique side table serves as a bedside night table, and its companion piece is a simple writing desk.

The focal point of the seating area, a gray fieldstone fireplace, is balanced by an oversize love seat and two comfortable chairs for lounging. As the design team explains, they decided on a sophisticated taupe chenille for the sofa because of its "softness and plushness." The club chair is upholstered in sophisticated toile, and an embossed leather wing chair is skirted with a silk trim.

Touches of chinoiserie are seen in the rich red hand-painted armoire that houses a television set and additional storage, and also in the intricate birch log pattern throughout the room, reminiscent of nineteenth-century frets and friezes.

The small screened porch located next to the bedroom suite, has a vibrantly painted red floor and is outfitted with a small table and chairs for intimate dining. A twig rocker sits in a corner by the window with a view of the treetops surrounding this tranquil cottage with its authentic Victorian touches.

LEFT Birch branches give the cottage a solid, natural wood interior without being dark and oppressive, allowing the designers to place dark pieces, such as the bed and side tables, in the room. The overall affect is awe-inspiring in its artistry and design. ABOVE A graceful bookcase.

TOP The crowning touch, a huge chandelier, looks part Chinese lantern, part eagle's nest. ABOVE A Victorian collection of egg specimens is one of the many delights tucked into the room. RIGHT Red touches are welcome in the otherwise black-and-white space. The delicate filigree of a birch-bark valance crown flanks a massive fieldstone fireplace.

RUSTIC CALM

Mecox Gardens in Bridgehampton, New York, on the eastern end of Long Island, is a must for gardening and design aficionados to visit. This charming shop specializes in mixing elements of garden and home decor and displaying them in imaginative and charming vignettes that illustrate not only how to blend antiques with new pieces but also how to mix in elements from outdoor gardens and porches.

Owner Mac Hoak has converted a former toolshed behind his shop into an enchanting bedroom cottage to showcase an eclectic collection of design treasures from around the world. Notes Hoak, "I used to live in a converted chicken coop so I do know something about living in rustic outdoorsy spaces!"

The exposed ceiling and the rough-hewn beams of the shed have been rubbed with a whitewash, and the interior walls are tinted a pale peach color, creating a welcoming setting for the muted tones of the pieces with which Hoak has filled the tiny room. His aesthetic: "I wanted to create a comfortable and

ABOVE A lovely juxtaposition of natural materials—a vintage cotton scalloped-edged sheet and an embroidered linen coverlet, a handblown glass vessel with gold rim and a lacquered wood tray on a seagrass table. OPPOSITE A water hyacinth root chair is set off by a traditional Kuba cloth decorative pillow.

casual feel with a sense of style, not overdone in any sense."

Throughout the skillfully appointed room, each piece is selected to enhance the rustic mood. Hoak chose a nineteenth-century campaign bed and covered it with a khaki linen coverlet and French cotton lace pillowcases. Hanging over the bed is a white Victorian cottage mirror circa 1890, and simply framed prints are placed on either side. Adding to the ambience, a pair of cube-shaped end tables covered in Normandy sea grass are topped with stylish necessities: one holds a tray, a decanter, a gold-rimmed cup, and a candelabrum; the other, a hurricane lamp and a vase filled with lilies.

On an adjacent wall, an English pine cupboard is a handsome and utilitarian storage space for linens and clothes. Next to the cupboard, a 1920s-style French bamboo desk is the setting for a stylish tableau. Beside the desk is a fragrant ginger plant in a large terra-cotta pot.

Hoak's calming bedroom design at Mecox mimics his own. "My bedroom is very casual, even rustic. With four large dogs in bed, it has to be relaxed. And it needs to be on the ground floor so you can walk right into the garden—bedrooms should have a connection to the outdoors."

SUMMER DACHA

amie Drake's visit to Versailles several years ago inspired a garden pavilion, dubbed the Folly, that the New York–based designer created in his Easthampton, Long Island, gardens. He recalls, "I visited Versailles on one of those rare weekends when all the water gardens are open to the public, and I decided then and there that I had to have a pavilion in my garden in the country."

When he got back to New York, Drake met with landscape and garden designer, Craig Socia, to ask for his help in designing and building the pavilion. It was the largest folly that Socia and his associates have attempted. "I showed Craig pictures of the pavilion I saw in Versailles. It had fancy gilding, which he didn't think would work," Drake says. "But he thought my backyard was perfect for a folly, and he immediately went to the drawing board."

The two-level rectangular pavilion that Socia crafted for Drake is constructed of eastern red cedar. Explains Socia: "Cedar has a great aroma; it keeps bugs away; it won't rot and it ages really well."

OPPOSITE The pavilion at twilight glows with the generous placement of candles, making it seem appropriate for a staging of *A Midsummer Night's Dream*. ABOVE Porthault's brilliantly colored pillow shams look like they were fashioned with cuttings from the garden. A timeless pattern, their fresh appeal is heightened in contrast to the nineteenth-century painted bed.

Socia says he looked at the folly as a work of art. "Most gazebos are fabricated and have a cookie-cutter look. With the follies I create for my clients, no two are alike."

Drake decided to create a bedroom in the folly because, he says, "After catching many guests napping in the cool shade, I decided the folly was the perfect opportunity to go one step further and create a wonderful bedroom for use in the deep heat of summer."

Drake started on the first level with a find from a local shop—a turn-of-the-century bed in sea green. A classic duvet in bright floral shades echoes the garden's summer hues.

Flush against the headboard, also an antique, is a simple table with a tin tray in bright hues that mimic the surroundings. A stack of books is nearby, because Drake says, "One of my favorite things to do out here is read in the quiet of nature." Adjacent to the bed is a twig basket stand filled with magazines and thick towels, ready for a guest who goes from the folly to a dip in the nearby pool.

For al fresco meals, a dining table and four chairs are arranged in a corner. Socia surprised his client with the custom-made Adirondack-style furniture (as well as a chaise, extra chairs, and cocktail tables) when the folly was completed. The designer decided on multifunctional pieces because, he says, "If I were going to use a folly, I'd want to be able to sit comfortably, stretch out and read a book, take a

OPPOSITE Electrical outlets in the pavilion are convenient for those times when candlelight just won't do. A monkey lamp looks natural in this setting. LEFT A single log was whittled to create a stairway that is "harmonious with the whole." A seating area upstairs is another delight, outfitted with cushioned twig seats and a small table. BELOW A twig plant stand works equally well to stow towels and magazines.

nap, and entertain friends." Drake added a touch of color and comfort to the furniture by covering the cushions in an all-weather fabric in another vibrant floral print.

The folly's upper level is an intimate space where Drake can sit and read, gaze at the sky above or at his colorful gardens below, or play cards with a guest.

A singular cedar log constitutes the staircase to the second level. It's a stunning feature and one that Socia deliberately set aside for this architectural element.

To complete the space, Socia and Drake decided upon a mixture of greenery to hang inside the folly and also to plant around it. Drake says, "I wanted a lush jungle-like feeling with a strong evergreen base that would stay verdant throughout the year. I love my ferns, and I can't wait until next year when the wisteria climbs over the roof."

Drake says he was thrilled to see the completed project, which took a team of seven men three weeks to complete. "We only built this folly a year ago," he says. "The plants are now close to maturity, so this is a dreamy space to come down to in the late afternoon for a nap or to enjoy cocktails with friends before ambling up to my terrace for a late summer dinner."

BALI MOODS

Imost every weekend from April to November, designer Todd Black leaves his Manhattan apartment for the small clapboard cottage he rents on Little Peconic Bay in Southampton, New York. For Black, who is also the lifestyle editor for *Hamptons Magazine,* his weekend house is his escape, his sanctuary. "It's quite isolated from the Hamptons scene," he says. "It's not about parties and restaurants; it's about the beach, friends, and quiet."

Black's intimate, exotic bedroom is, he notes, "oriented toward the water view of beach and bay. Nothing is better than napping here with the sun setting outside the window. I've even hung a hammock outside the room to truly capitalize on it. Inside, the dogs monopolize the sofa as their place to nap, but I have my desk out here and I've found it's a great place to work, hearing the water and feeling the sea breezes. This place, for me, is otherworldly."

Since Black rents his weekend home, he was somewhat restricted in his design options. The walnut-finished wood paneling in the bedroom, for example, could not be changed, but he could use

ABOVE With the blue of the bay in the background, Black relaxes with Wallis on a hammock just outside his bedroom door. OPPOSITE Black brings the large banana leaves from his favorite florist in Manhattan. They can last for many weeks. A laptop is a reminder that time here is not all play.

LEFT Wallis contentedly hangs out on the bed, waiting for his afternoon swim. A sculptural Isamu Noguchi lamp is almost as tall as the ceiling, and at night it offers light as yet another textural element. A conch shell on the night table is actually of carved wood, found in the Philippines.

textures and accessories imaginatively. "I've used fabrics and other tones throughout the bedroom to get a depth that you normally wouldn't get with paneling. I love to play with textures—it adds a wonderful warmth to any room."

The bed—"essentially an unremarkable bed," Black notes—came with the house. "So I covered the headboard with a khaki cotton," he says, "and for my bed skirt I chose burlap, which I also used on the window treatments." The geometric pattern works well in the room. The comforter and blanket, khaki and rust-colored, were designed by Black's friend and college roommate, John Robshaw, while the raw silk shams and sheets are from Ralph Lauren. Black chose the muted color scheme for his bedding and accessories because "they are soothing and calming," he says. "The colors reflect the beach environment. They are the same tone as the outdoors, and they work with the paneling."

The desk—writing table also came with the house. "Again, it's nothing special, but the base has some character, so I covered it with a black and khaki sarong I found in Saint Barts," says Black. The director's chair evokes memories, as it came from a forty-five-foot sailboat docked in Sag Harbor where Black lived before he began renting this house.

The desk is strewn with objects Black has collected over the years: African masks found at a street fair in Manhattan, a watercolor from a flea market, an antique bronze fish, and a collection of shells from his beach walks.

Scattered pieces throughout the room reinforce the ambience of a beachfront bedroom and are practical at the same time. These include straw floor mats from Pier I,

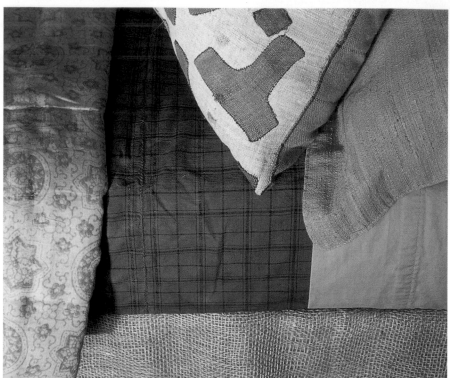

RIGHT The burlap bedskirt matches the curtain on the sliding glass door. The comforter and blanket from friend John Robshaw are based on traditional Southeast Asian design. The front pillow is made from African kuba cloth. BELOW A still life above a built-in storage unit. OPPOSITE The Bernice desk lamp is an Italian modern classic.

hurricane candles, and a collection of straw hats for friends to wear on the beach.

Black's two Jack Russell terriers often accompany him to his beach house. Eight-year-old Wallis and Winston love the setting as much as their owner does. But, says Black, "when we're outside, it's hard to keep them out of the bay."

Black considers his bedroom "my own little piece of heaven. It's about sand and dogs and flopping on the bed for a nap fresh from a swim in the bay."

"A bedroom," muses Black, "should be the most personal room in a home and should be most reflective of its owner. I really believe it should serve lots of functions—not just as a place to sleep but also as a refuge where you can shut out the world. It is a space to do not only what you need to do but also what you want to do."

HARBOR MORNINGS

hen Karen and Bill Tell of Greenwich, Connecticut, moved to a waterfront home, they enlisted designer Sandy Morgan to help them create a setting that would reflect their love of the sea.

Their bedroom, which faces the harbor, was a particular challenge for Sandy. "My clients wanted the room to work both as a sleeping room and a sitting room," she recalls. "They also didn't want the interior elements to compete with the incredible water views. I wanted to open this room to the special light that comes in off the sea, but also to balance it so that it wouldn't overwhelm the room."

To soften the afternoon light, Morgan chose a sheer printed chintz from Cowtan & Tout to create a soft and glossy screen of curtains. A rattan armoire serves as home to the television set while providing additional storage space.

The bed, with its upholstered headboard, is situated to enjoy the harbor views. Sandy has dressed it with white cotton sheets with

OPPOSITE From the deck, a view of the seating area inside. The Moroccan table was purchased abroad. The blond armoire is from the Brighton Pavilion Collection for Ficks Reed. ABOVE On the deck, an old-fashioned porch swing invites quiet reflection or bird-watching in the waterway when the tide is out.

"When the doors are open to the outdoors,

shell-pink embroidery that the Tells bought in Egypt. Draping the bed is a handsome soft pink down comforter with a scalloped edge from Lynnens of Greenwich, one of Morgan's favorite shops. For her book-loving clients, Morgan had bookshelf niches, with closed cabinets below, built on either side of the bed. Swing-arm Hansen lamps provide reading light on both sides of the bed.

Notes Morgan, "When the doors are open to the outdoors, the translucent curtains blow in the breeze and open to the almost ethereal view." Karen agrees. "This bedroom reminds me of Nantucket," she says, "because of the incredible bird life right outside our bedroom window. Shore birds like egrets, ospreys, and kingfishers are widely prevalent. When they migrate from Nantucket to Greenwich, it's like my friends are visiting."

BELOW Swing-arm Hanson lamps installed on the built-in shelf, rather than flat on the wall, are a practical design solution. At the end of the bed sits a reproduction Louis XIV bench upholstered in an informal plaid. RIGHT The antique pine-and-rush chair from Wales was originally a nursing chair, the back curved to keep drafts off the baby.

the translucent curtains blow in the breeze."

THE OVERLOOK

ocated offshore of New England, the Anchorage is a summer "cottage" in the grand old tradition of summer cottages —three stories of white-painted shingles, ample porches, gabled windows, large fireplaces, and enough nooks and crannies to satisfy the most romantically inclined.

Off the second-floor master bedroom, protected by the eaves and the massive fieldstones of the chimney, a tiny open porch is tucked. It is here that the lady of the house can enjoy a private moment, a respite from the comings and goings of children and grandchildren heading for the beach or the sailboats, preparing to play tennis or golf, or making forays to the kitchen for snacks.

"This porch is all about her," says Sarah Smith, an interior designer from New York City who planned the space for her client. "The couple who own the Anchorage live in Maryland. She grew up summering on the island so it was natural that she should return here with her own family. This is her retreat, her one totally private place in this large family dwelling."

ABOVE Antique lace pillows and a nineteenth-century appliqué floral quilt dress the "bed." OPPOSITE Prize-winning pink and yellow dahlias from the garden and an antique red watering can are a vibrant contrast to the blue of the bay.

the abcs of bedding

The design element that first grabs your attention in all great bedrooms is the way the bed is dressed. Bed linens speak as clearly about a room as clothes speak about the people who wear them. A simple change of linens—in the way they are layered or in their texture, color, or design—can alter the mood of the room from formal to funky, from rustic to romantic, or from sleek and modern to frilly and old-fashioned.

The volume of bedding and how you arrange it on the bed can also indicate your design proclivities. Do you favor mounds of lush pillows and piles of down, or do you prefer the streamlined simplicity of a classic blanket and a single pillow? Do you make your bed the way you were taught, with a spread pulled up and over the pillows and sliced into a clean line underneath them, or do you experiment and play with bedding the way you do your personal fashion accessories?

No matter what your style or how you choose to make your bed, linens and bedding should reflect your personality and your unique design sensibilities. As illustrated by the bedrooms photographed in this book, here are some ideas to help you define your own style.

ROMANTIC ELEGANCE

Unite the elements of the room with wall covering, window fabrics, a skirted table, and upholstered furniture in the same floral or toile pattern. Dress the bed in classic tailored linens of fine fabric. A bedspread in a matching toile also works well, but exercise restraint with some fabrics. If you use too much of the same thing, you will risk the hotel-room look. Luxurious throws in wool or cashmere, added trims of pom-poms or a simple lace complete the romantic look.

ARCHITECTURAL INFLUENCES

Keep linens, bedding, and other furnishings minimal to emphasize the light and space of an architecturally significant room. Use white or monochromatic linens and pillows and fabrics that rely on texture instead of color for their effectiveness.

COUNTRY MOODS

Country rooms are relaxed and homey. Celebrate your country roots by incorporating cabin style, farmhouse style, or seaside charm. For the country look coordinate new or vintage quilts, camp blankets, and comforters. Mix and match ginghams, stripes, checks, plaids, and florals in your sheet patterns. Pile on the vintage pillows. Mix Grandmother's antique linens with those you picked up at a tag sale or outlet store.

GUEST HAVENS

Guest rooms should be calm and serene, an inviting home away from home that comforts without distracting. Choose fabrics and linens in the same color. Coordinate calming shades such as beige, tan, or white with soft pale blue, yellow, or green. Keep the guest room uncluttered, but provide plenty of pillows, in different sizes and fabrics, bearing in mind that some guests may be allergic to down. Put an extra blanket at the end of the bed and more in a closet or storage area.

CHILDREN'S HOUR

For children's rooms, play up a theme that suits your child's personality or interests while bearing in mind that those interests will change over the years. To inspire good bed-making habits, avoid fussy beds strewn with lots of pillows and toys. Keep things simple, with cozy comforters, coordinated pillows, and soft sheets in solid muted colors or stripes. Save the cartoon characters, sports figures, and ballerinas for the books on the shelves or the items in the toy chest.

NATURE'S WAY

Select themes from nature as a motif for your fabrics and bed linens. Look for fabrics that feature wood grains, leaves, or botanicals. Coordinate the bed with nubby textures, raw cotton, and silk or burlap, with fabrics that look homespun or handmade, such as grass cloth, materials printed with natural dyes, or Kuba cloth. Ethnic prints and fabrics work well with the colors found in nature—browns, greens, beiges, and vibrant floral colors.

A GOOD NIGHT

A well-dressed bed can set the style of your room, yet all the style in the world cannot guarantee a restful night. A good mattress and box spring can. A mattress is not just the stuffing for your sheets; it is the platform upon which you spend about a third of your life, affecting not just the way you sleep, but also how you feel in the morning and throughout your day. It is time to consider your bed in its naked state.

If you decide that you need a new mattress and box spring, do your research before you buy. You need to test your options and talk to an experienced mattress salesperson. Shop in comfortable clothing that approximates your pajamas and don't be shy about getting into bed, with your partner, in the middle of a showroom. What you're looking for in a good mattress is a good inner spring unit that is composed of individual steel coils placed inside the mattress shell. These, depending on the quality, price, and style, may be tied together, placed in fabric pockets, or made of one continuous steel wire that is formed into coils. The coil count is the number of coils in the mattress. The more coils, presumably, the higher the quality and the price, but also the better the mattress can respond to changing sleep positions.

Once you've mastered the coil question, the next consideration is whether to get one of the new pillowtop mattresses or settle for a plush or regular mattress. Pillowtop mattresses can make your bed reach lofty new heights of comfort, but you may also need a ladder just to climb into bed, and deep-pocket fitted sheets to accommodate the extra thickness. The pillowtop has a separate layer of padding sewn to both the top and bottom, which looks as if it can be lifted off. It can't. But the extra padding eases the pressure points at the hips and shoulders, ensuring a more comfortable night's rest. A plush mattress is not as thick as a pillowtop, but it does have extra layers of plush padding over the coils, sewn under the mattress shell. A regular mattress lacks all the extra padding but is comfortable for the short term. It's all you need in a crib mattress, or a bunk bed that will be outgrown in the span of childhood, or your first bed before you upgrade to a queen or king.

Turning your mattress on a regular basis, end to end and side to side, is important to prolong its life and avoid telltale body impressions. It is recommended that you flip a new mattress once a month for six months and once every season thereafter. If mattress flipping is no sport for you, consider a one-sided no-flip mattress. These are constructed on a special foundation with high-density foam and individually wrapped coils. Expect to pay extra for the privilege.

Now let's consider the fabric covering, or ticking. If you intend to buy only one mattress and box spring set in your lifetime, you may do well to consider a mattress covered with Belgian damask, or a fabric of cashmere, silk, or fine wool, with a lifetime warranty. These coverings are not merely luxurious, they are also incredibly durable, able to withstand a lifetime of use. Mattresses with a lifetime warranty are usually constructed with twenty-four-karat gold corner guards and layers of latex and visco foam, cotton, and other natural fibers, including cashmere and wool, over the inner coils.

Consider a hypoallergenic ticking if you are allergy-prone. Mattress ticking made of a cotton-polyester blend works well in children's rooms, since it is washable and more waterproof, as well as for adult beds when the lifetime warranty model is not an option.

Mattresses and box springs are often sold separately, but it is generally true that if you need to replace one you should replace the other. Buying a set usually offers a cost savings, as well. Box springs are fairly standard, considering all the options for mattresses. But a poorer quality mattress will make life harder for the box spring and vice versa—a good mattress will ease the demands on the box spring.

Have a very good night.

resources

The special places that can help make your bedroom inviting, comfortable, and beautiful are endless. With treasures such as hand-me-downs, gifts, flea-market finds, and bedding purchases from specialty shops and department stores, we design the most private room in our homes. I love to browse at all different types of shops to create a personal look, and I've compiled a list of some of my favorite places. I've also included shops I've been told are fabulous shopping experiences.

You'll notice many antiques stores in this list. That's because I've always loved antiques and vintage pieces, and one of the best places to showcase them is in the bedroom—whether it's an old English wrought-iron bed piled high with Victorian linens or a dressing table that says Art Deco. And I couldn't leave out my favorite places to find rare books, because the bedroom is where I love to store my ever-growing book collection. I hope this list of resources helps you as you create or add to your own unique and personal bedroom.

Shops and Services

Didier Aaron
32 East 67th Street
New York, NY 10021
(212) 988-5248
www.didieraaron.com

ABC Carpet and Home
888 Broadway
New York, NY 10003
(212) 473-3000

Aero
132 Spring Street
New York, NY 10012
(212) 966-4700

Alexander Gallery
942 Madison Avenue
New York, NY 10021
(212) 517-4400

Alice's Antiques
72 Green Street
New York, NY 10012
(212) 874-3400

America Hurrah Antiques
230 Central Park West
New York, NY 10021
(212) 535-1930

Anichini, Inc.
230 Fifth Avenue, Suite 1900
New York, NY 10001
(800) 553-5309
www.anichini.com

Ann Morris Antiques
239 East 60th Street
New York, NY 10022
(212) 755-3308

Anthropologie
(800) 309-2500
www.anthropologie.com

W. Graham Arader III
29 East 72nd Street
New York, NY 10021
(212) 628-3668

Balasses House Antiques
Main Street
Amagansett, NY 11930
(516) 267-3032

Bardith
901 Madison Avenue
New York, NY 10021
(212) 737-3775

Bassett Furniture
PO Box 626
Bassett, VA 24055
(540) 629-6000
www.bassettfurniture.com

Bed, Bath & Beyond
650 Liberty Avenue
Union, NJ 07083
(800) GO-BEYOND
www.bedbathandbeyond
.com

Bellora
(718) 747-1656

Bloomingdale's
1000 Third Avenue
New York, NY 10022
(212) 705-2000

Yale R. Burge
315 East 63 Street
New York, NY 10021
(212) 838-4005

Carriage Trade
    Antique Center
190 Main Street Center
Manchester, VT 05255
(802) 362-1125

Chambers
(800) 334-1254

Chelsea Antiques
14 West Putnam Avenue
Greenwich, CT 06830
(212) 699-1023

Cherishables Antiques
1608 20 Street NW
Washington, DC 20009
(202) 785-4087

Crane Collection
121 Newbury Street
Boston, MA 02116
(617) 262-4080

Crate and Barrel
(800) 996-9960
(800) 323-5461 (catalog)
www.crateandbarrel.com

Country Gear
2408 Main Street
PO Box 727
Bridgehampton, NY 11932
(631) 537-7069

Donghia
979 Third Avenue, Suite 613
New York, NY 10022
(212) 935-3713
www.donghia.com

Door Store
One Park Avenue
New York, NY 10021
(212) 679-9700
www.doorstorefurniture.com

D. Porthault Linens & Co.
18 East 69th Street
New York, NY 10021
(212) 688-1661

Eddie Bauer Home
PO Box 97000
Redmond, WA
    98073-9700
(800) 426-8020
www.eddiebauer.com

Evergreen Antiques
1249 Third Avenue
New York, NY 10021
(212) 744-5664
www.evergreenantiques.com

EXPO Design Center
877 Franklin Road
Marietta, GA 30067
(678) 581-8500
www.homedepot.com

Fortunoff
1300 Old Country Road
Westbury, NY 11590
(516) 832-9000
www.fortunoff.com

French Laundry Ltd.
240 Peachtree Street NW,
    Suite 9B1
Atlanta, GA 30303
(404) 524-8040

Frette
799 Madison Avenue
New York, NY 10021
(212) 988-5221

Garnet Hill
262 Main Street
Franconia, NH 03580
(800) 622-6216
www.garnethill.com

George Subkoff Antiques
643 Danbury Road,
    Route 7
Wilton, CT 06897
(203) 834-0703

Georgica Creek Antiques
PO Box 877
Wainscott, NY 11975
(631) 537-0333

G.K.S. Bush Antiques
2828 Pennsylvania Avenue
    NW
Washington, DC 20007
(202) 965-0653

Price Glover
59 East 79th Street
New York, NY 10021
(212) 772-1740

Hammacher Schlemmer
147 East 57th Street
New York, NY 10022
(212) 421-9000

Hilary House
86 Chestnut Street
Boston, MA 02108
(617) 523-7118

Homer
939 Madison Avenue
New York, NY 10021
(212) 744-7705
www.homerdesign.com

The Horchow Collection
PO Box 620048
Dallax, TX 75262-0048
(800) 456-7000
www.neimanmarcus.com

Ruth Hubbell
2106 Thell Road
Rye, NY 10580
(914) 967-7275

Judy Hubener
Waterworks
PO Box 2364
Manchester, VT 05255
(802) 362-2975
www.waterworks.com

The Hudson
  Antiques Center
536 Warren Street
Hudson, NY 12534
(518) 828-9920

Hyde Park Antiques
836 Broadway
New York, NY 10003
(212) 477-0033

IKEA
1000 IKEA Center Way
Elizabeth, NJ 07201
(908) 289-4498
www.ikea.com

Indigo Seas
123 North Robertson
  Boulevard
Los Angeles, CA 90048
(310) 550-8758

Jansen Antiques
1042 Pine Street
Philadelphia, PA 19107
(215) 922-5594

JC Penney
One Lincoln Center,
  Fourteenth Floor
PO Box 10001
Dallas, TX 75301-7207
(800) 222-6161
www.jcpenney.com

John Rosselli Antiques
523 East 73rd Street
New York, NY 10021
(212) 772-2137

Greg Jordan
504 East 74th Street,
  Fourth Floor
New York, NY 10021
(212) 570-4470

Kentshire Galleries
37 East 12th Street
New York, NY 10003
(212) 673-6644

Kinderhook Antique Center
Route 9H
Kinderhook, NY 12106
(518) 758-7939

Lands' End
5 Lands' End Lane
Dodgeville, WI 53595
(800) 356-4444
www.landsend.com

Laura Ashley
6 St. James Avenue,
  Tenth Floor
Boston, MA 02116
(800) 367-2000
www.Laura-Ashleyusa.com

Leron
750 Madison Avenue
New York, NY 10021
(212) 249-3188
www.leron.com

Linen Source
5401 Hangar Court
Tampa, FL 33631-3151
www.linensource.com

L.L. Bean
Freeport, ME 04033
(800) 221-4221
www.llbean.com

Longoria Collection
1101-02 Uptown Park
  Boulevard
Houston, TX 77056
(713) 621-4241

Lowe's Home Centers Inc.
PO Box 1111
North Wilkesboro, NC
  28656-0001
(800) 445-6937

Lynnens
278 Greenwich Avenue
Greenwich, CT 06830
(203) 629-3659
www.lynnens.com

Mary Farrell Homeside
  Building Corporation
166 Old Mamaroneck Road
White Plains, NY 10605

Mecox Gardens
257 County Road 39A
Southampton, NY 11968
(631) 287-5015
www.mecoxgardens.com

Millbrook Antiques Mall
PO Box 1267
Franklin Avenue
Millbrook, NY 12545
(914) 677-9311

Mohawk Industries, Inc.
PO Box 130
Sugar Valley, GA 30746
www.mohawkind.com

Tom Molloy, Renovator
42 Dillingham Avenue
Manchester, VT 05254

Nancy Stanley Ward
  Fine Linens
8918 Burton Way, No. 4
Beverly Hills, CA 90211
(310) 273-3690
(310) 273-3691 (fax)

Nellie's of Amagansett
230 Main Street
PO Box 2790
Amagansett, NY 11930

Nesle
151 East 57th Street
New York, NY 10022
(212) 755-0515
www.dir-dd.com/nesle.html

Newel Galleries
425 East 53rd Street
New York, NY 10022
(212) 758-1970
www.newel.com

N. Keen & Co.
3609 Historic Route 7A
Manchester, VT 05254
(802) 366-8036

The Old Print Shop
150 Lexington Avenue
New York, NY 10016
(212) 683-3950
www.oldprintshop.com

Old World Craftsmen
38 Perry Avenue
Port Chester, NY 10573
(914) 937-0347

Orkney and Yost Antiques
148 Water Street
Stonington, CT 06378
(203) 642-7226

Paper White Ltd.
1011 Magnolia Ave.
Larkspur, CA 94939
(415) 925-1540

Florian Papp
962 Madison Avenue
New York, NY 10021
(212) 288-6770
www.florianpapp.com

The Pawling Antique Center
22 Charles Coleman
  Boulevard
Pawling, NY 12564
(914) 855-3611

Pier 1 Imports
225 Greenwich Avenue
Greenwich, CT 06830
(800) 245-4595
www.pier1.com

Pierre Deux
870 Madison Avenue
New York, NY 10021
(212) 570-9343
www.pierredeux.com

Pierre Deux Antiques
369 Bleecker Street
New York, NY 10014
(212) 243-7740

Pottery Barn
(800) 922-5507
www.potterybarn.com

Pratesi
829 Madison Avenue
New York, NY 10021
(212) 288-2315

Property
14 Wooster Street
New York, NY 10013
(917) 237-0123

Ralph Lauren Home Stores
650 Madison Avenue
New York, NY 10026
(212) 318-7000
www.PoloRalphLauren.com

James Robinson
480 Park Avenue
New York, NY 10022
(212) 752-6166

Rue de France
78 Thames Street
Newport, RI 02840
(800) 777-0998

Sallea Antiques
120 Main Street
New Canaan, CT 06840
(203) 972-1938

David A. Schorsch
1037 North Street
Greenwich, CT 06831
(203) 869-8797

Schweitzer Linens
457 Columbus Avenue
New York, NY 10024
(212) 799-9629

Seabrook Wallcoverings
1325 Farmville Road
Memphis, TN 38122
(800) 238-9152
www.seabrookwall
   coverings.com

Sears
3333 Beverly Road
Hoffman Estates, IL 60179
(800) 549-4505

Simply French
2487 Main Street
PO Box 9000
Bridgehampton, NY 11932
(631) 537-7444

Sleepy's
Robert Jennings
1340 East Putnam Avenue
Old Greenwich, CT 06870
(718) 547-2161
(203) 637-8571

Sleepy's
440 Park Avenue South
New York, NY 10016
(212) 725-1492

Smith & Noble
PO Box 1838
Corona, CA 92878-9933
www.smithandnoble.com

Stock Market
Post Road
Southport, CT 06903

Stubbs and Wooten
22 East 72nd Street
New York, NY 10021
(212) 249-5200

Sturbridge Antique Shops
128 Charlton Road,
   Route 20
Sturbridge, MA 01566
(508) 347-2744

Sussex Antiques
PO Box 796
Bedford, NY 10506
(914) 241-2919
By appointment

Target Stores
PO Box 1392
Minneapolis, MN
   55440-1392
(800) 440-0680
www.target.com

Todd Romano Antiques
   and Decorating
157 East 71st Street
New York, NY 10021
(212) 879-7722

Michael Trapp
7 River Road
West Cornwall, CT 06796
(860) 672-6098

Treillage
418 East 75th Street
New York, NY 10021
(212) 535-2288

Ursus Books and Prints
981 Madison Avenue
New York, NY 10021
(212) 772-8787
www.ursusbooks.com

VW Home
333 West 39th Street,
   Tenth Floor
New York, NY 10018
(212) 244-5008

Washington Square Gallery
221 Chestnut Street
Philadelphia, PA 19106
(215) 923-8873

The Whale's Rib
Cranberry Island, MA

Whispering Pines Catalog
43 Ruane Street
Fairfield, CT 06430
(203) 259-5027
(203) 259-5041 (fax)
www.whisperingpines
   catalog.com

Jamson Whyte
47 Wooster Street
New York, NY 10013
(212) 965-9405

Wicker Garden
1327 Madison Avenue
New York, NY 10128
(212) 410-7000

Woodard & Greenstein
Woodard Weave Classic
   American Woven Rugs
506 East 74th Street,
   Fifth Floor
New York, NY 10021
(212) 988-2906
www.woodardweave.com

Designers and Architects

Warren and Mai Arthur
316 Grove Street
New Canaan, CT 06840
(203) 966-5528

Danielle Austin
721 Ridgefield Road
Wilton, CT 06897
(203) 834-8501

Penny Drue Baird
787 Madison Avenue,
    Third Floor
New York, NY 10021
(212) 288-3600

Todd Black
33 Riverside Drive,
    Suite 5B
New York, NY 10023
(212) 875-0014

Chris Coleman
70 Washington Street
Brooklyn, NY 11201
(718) 222-8984

Craig James Socia
    Garden Design
PO Box 2739
Easthampton, NY 11937
(631) 324-8741

Ellie Cullman
790 Madison Avenue
New York, NY 10021
(212) 249-3874

James D'Auria
20 West 36th Street,
    Twelfth Floor
New York, NY 10018
(212) 268-1142

Jamie Drake
140 East 56th Street,
    Suite 4J
New York, NY 10022
(212) 754-3099

Mark Finlay
1300 Post Road, Suite 101
Fairfield, CT 06430
(203) 254-2388

Toni Gallagher
10 Thistle Lane
Rye, NY 10580
(914) 967-7609

Glenn Gissler
36 East 22nd Street,
    Eighth Floor
New York, NY 10010
(212) 228-9880

Karen Houghton
41 North Broadway
Nyack, NY 10960
(914) 358-0133

Sandy Morgan
31 Brookside Drive
Greenwich, CT 06830
(203) 629-8121

Arlene Pilson
45 Cradle Rock Road
Pound Ridge, NY 10576
(914) 764-4747

Cindy Rinfret
165 West Putnam Avenue,
    Second Floor
Greenwich, CT 06830

Carolyn Schultz
429 Forest Avenue
Rye, NY 10580
(914) 967-3601

Sarah Smith
152 East 79th Street
New York, NY 10021
(212) 327-4371

Matthew Smyth
135 East 65th Street
New York, NY 10021
(212) 333-5353

Stephanie Stokes
139 East 57th Street
New York, NY 10022
(212) 756-9922

Twin Farms Inn
Stage Road
Barnard, VT 05031
(800) 234-9999

Barrie Vanderpoel
79 East 79th Street
New York, NY 10121
(212) 472-0405

Helene Verin
21 East 22nd Street,
    Room 2C
New York, NY 10010
(212) 533-5154

index